Theatre and Europe: 1957-95

Christopher McCullough

intellect™

intellect

EUROPEAN STUDIES SERIES

General Editor: *Keith Cameron*

First Published in 1996 by
Intellect Books
EFAE, Earl Richards Road North, Exeter EX2 6AS, UK

Series editor:	Keith Cameron
Production:	Rachel Carey, Alison Smith
Copy editor:	Judith Wise

British Library Cataloguing in Publication Data Available

ISBN 1-871516-82-X

Printed and bound in Great Britain by Cromwell Press, Wiltshire

Contents

Preface

Theatre and Europe is concerned with the matter of post-war Europe and its cultural identity as manifest through the variety of its theatrical activity. It is not a survey in the conventional sense, nor is it an in-depth study of a particular group of individuals or genres of theatre. What is attempted, in the first instance, is an over view of the main strands of European thought regarding the range of development of post-war European consciousness. This approach is then advanced by attention to significant moments of theatre practice. The selected practitioners are represented because they serve as appropriate 'signposts' by which we may understand how a particular moment of disruption (or indeed celebration) was manifest in the development of post-war European culture. It is important to recognise the distinction that may be drawn between culture in its evaluative and in its analytic sense. *Theatre and Europe* lays greater emphasis on the analytic sense of the term, wishing to illuminate a particular moment when theatre may be seen as an expression of, or a moment of subversion in, the accepted cultural status quo.

As examples, we may consider the inclusion of Jean-Louis Barrault and his involvement in the Paris student demonstrations of the late 1960s, in relation to the reshaping of left-wing political ideologies after the Soviet interventions in Hungary and Czechoslovakia. Equally, *The Playwrights' Manifesto* of 1980 reveals an anxiety about the perceived displacement of the writer and the pre-eminence of the literary form of drama in the face of theatre companies that sought to place the creative efforts of actors at the centre of theatre making.

Theatre and Europe attempts to address a debate about the ways by which we may begin to understand how culture is made. The contention is that theatre may no longer be perceived as separate from (that is transcendent of) the material conditions of production.

While not claiming to be a thorough survey of post-war European theatre, *Theatre and Europe* aims to instigate a debate from which the student of theatre may be enabled to develop further in her or his own investigations. It should be seen as a tool, or a starting point, rather than as a definitive commodity to be taken at face value. There are no answers in the book, simply an attempt to raise certain questions regarding the relationship of theatre to the sense of ourselves as Europeans.

Introduction

It is often argued that the evolution of the concept of post Second World War Europe arises as much from the political machinations of the USA, Britain and France with their need to control the sovereignty of Germany with the aim to present a 'united' front to the emergent threat of the Soviet Union, as from the wish to realise the ideals of a common cultural heritage. One very practical outcome of the Second World War was, that while Britain, France and Germany in essence had lost their nineteenth-century empires, the Soviet Union and the United States of America emerged as the two super powers, replacing the old European empires and their spheres of influence around the world.

Within Europe the impetus, from the break-up of the Holy Roman Empire (which was in itself a medieval attempt to retain, under a Christian ideology, the unity provided by the Roman Empire) was towards the growth of the nation state. The political boundaries, to a large extent, were determined by the ideological split between Protestantism and Roman Catholicism. By the end of the First World War, the nation state was the dominant pattern shaping the map of Europe. The creativity embodied in literature, music and the other performing arts existed, in the view of Hegel, as an expression of the nation's 'folk genius', denying the idea of a common European heritage and favouring the development of art as the expression of national sovereignty.

The Treaty of Rome to the Entry of the United Kingdom: 1957 – The Beginnings of Unity

The idea of European unity in the inter-war years was remote and restricted to the thoughts of a few visionaries marginalised by the hegemony of nationalism. As early as 1930 the French foreign minister, Aristide Briand, had prepared a memorandum for a united Europe, but events that offered an undesired form of European unity overtook such proposals in 1939.

The desires of post-war 'Europeanists' such as Winston Churchill, Pope Pius XII, Paul-Henri Spaak, Alcide de Gasperi, Robert Schuman, and Konrad Adenauer, although various in their motives, were to avoid intra-European war and to promote the compelling economic arguments for co-operation. They perceived that the success of the North American economy was due, in no small part, to the size of their internal market.

The first major step towards integration was taken in 1947 when the United States asked for the establishment of a common European organisation to plan the distribution of American aid under what has become known as the *Marshall plan*. This plan offered the possibility of forestalling a severe post-war economic crisis with seventeen nations co-ordinating activities under the organisation for European Economic Co-operation (OEEC). However, this may be seen as a false start. The East European nations, under Stalin's pressure, refused to take part as the membership was international, rather than supranational, with the USA as a member.

The second major step towards Europeanisation was in 1948 with the formation of the Congress of Europe, which in turn led to the formation of the Council of Europe, the intention of which was to plan the possible integration of Europe. Resistance was immediately apparent, particularly from Britain. Fearing for the relationship with the trading partners of the Commonwealth and perceiving the open anti-Sovietism of the Council, Britain signed the agreement with extreme reluctance. A result of British opposition meant that the Council's power was limited to recommendation only without any real power of deliberation.

For those active members of the Council, the development of the Cold War fuelled the need for greater economic and political union, in order to oppose any thrust into Western Europe by the emergent Soviet Bloc. In 1949 the Soviet Union exploded its first atomic weapon, increasing the general sense of insecurity in Western Europe. The final impulse towards some kind of unification came with the involvement of the USA in Korea. With US troops engaged in the Far East, nominally as a part of a United Nations force, the American government was pressurising the Western European states to re-arm Germany as a bulwark against potential Soviet expansionism.

France, having perhaps the greatest sense of insecurity, took the lead in promoting the negotiations that led towards the setting up, in 1952, of the European Coal and Steel Community (ESC). It was seen that Germany would not remain weak and so the only alternative was to draw Germany into an economic union, making war an entirely counterproductive step for all involved. Britain refused to join for what seem to be depressingly familiar reasons, involving close ties with the USA and Commonwealth and an unwillingness to sacrifice any sense of national sovereignty. This state of affairs kept Britain and the membership of the EEC at bay for the next twenty years. This cultural and economic separation was, and still is a marked distinction between Britain and the rest of Europe. It may be argued that Britain's reputation for the arts (in particular theatre) in the post-war years has been parasitical; the richness and power of theatre in Britain resting entirely on what has been acquired from French (Existentialism), German (Expressionism, Brecht and Marxism), Italian (Futurism), Soviet Union (Meyerhold and Constructivism) and much more thought and experimentation, while retaining an essentially conservative view of what theatre should be.

The most important point in the development of European collaboration was in the signing of the Treaty of Rome in 1957 and thus the establishment of the European Economic Community; to which of course Britain made its belated entry in 1972. In 1950 the USA had attempted to force the Western European states into what would have become the European Defence Community, but this was an issue fraught with problems and which found its demise in the early 1950s with the death of Stalin and the end of the Korean war.

A much generalised analysis might argue that the political and economic distance between Britain and the rest of Europe is part of the same structural relationship as is its cultural distance. Obviously there is the common Judeo/Christian cultural heritage, but there is still the sense, at least in the mythology that constitutes a large part of British thinking, that Britain is different from all those countries that constitute the continent of Europe.

Obvious constituent parts to the argument would have to include the Protestant Reformation in England and the growth of the British Empire. The Reformation itself was a part of the emergence of English Nationalism (although Nationalism in the sixteenth century was not unknown among Roman Catholics and Nationalism only really became synonymous with Protestantism after the death of Henry VIII) emerging as it did in the 1530s with the anti-Papal, anti-clerical, Anglican and Erastian tide of revolution. From then on the (cultural) separation of England from the rest of Europe developed and was fed by the development of the British Empire and its proselytising belief in the advantages of being 'British'. I place British in quotation marks for the obvious reason that the 'British' Empire was, to a large extent, the English Empire. The intention is not to marginalise England's Celtic neighbours, but to highlight the fact that most power is centred in London and that, certainly in the sixteenth century, Ireland and Scotland were as much potential Catholic threats to the 'new' nation of England, as were France and Spain.

Cultural Directions in Post-War Europe

It is often argued that an all-pervasive cultural pessimism swept over Europe in the aftermath of the Second World War. The mass extermination of peoples, the bombing of civilian centres and the atomic bombing of Japan, left Europeans with a distrust in the inevitable progress of history and an uncertainty about the existence of tomorrow. Except for the alternative ideological perspectives offered by the various theoretical views of Marxism, which were and are disparate, the areas of artistic endeavour that dominated Europe evolved in the questions raised by modernism. For the post-war generation, all ideological systems, facts, and rational knowledge in all likelihood could, and perhaps would, inevitably lead to the destruction of civilisation; if indeed such a term still possessed any significant currency.

This fragmentation of the perception of history cannot be limited to the aftermath of the Second World War, indeed it may be argued that the vision was disrupted more severely by the events surrounding the First World War. The two main ideological thrusts in the arts, and in particular theatre, developed in the inter-war years. In the first instance we may identify the particular development from modernism and existential philosophy that declared itself in the notion of the 'absurd' and in the transcendental and often quasi-mystical experiments of directors who sought a unifying 'inter-cultural' role for theatre in so-called anthropological studies. Alternatively, there is what we might term the 'materialist' route. This approach is derived from Marxist philosophy and more directly and even pragmatically, from Bertolt Brecht. In Britain the materialist influence has perhaps been most strongly observed in the work of groups loosely conjoined under the socialist banner and even within liberal institutions such as the Royal Shakespeare Company.

The situation is complex and if a central task of this volume is to comment on the variety of aspects of European theatre practice, it is vital that we locate those practices within the broad context of European thought. In order to explain this premise, a brief survey of philosophical developments in post-First World War Europe may help towards a fuller contextualisation of the development of European theatre practice.

Existentialism

In many senses existentialism was an appropriate response to the aftermath of the Second World War and it may be argued that it was no accident of fate that the clearest manifestation of the philosophical argument took place in France, a country not only occupied, but also fought on, and consequently a culture having every reason to question its sense of isolation from its historic metaphysical and transcendental roots.

Although existentialism as a system of thought was formulated long before the Second World War in the work of Kierkegaard, Nietzsche and Heidegger, the acceptance and embracing of it by the *literati* largely took place in the 1940s and 1950s. Perhaps, rather than a philosophy in the strictest sense of the term, Existentialism became one of the ways of dealing with the problems of living in the middle of the twentieth century. We find a rejection of all systems based upon a mechanistic understanding of the universe, with the concept of the absurd perhaps exemplified in Albert Camus' essay *Le Mythe de Sisyphe*. Sisyphus was condemned by the gods to a task of futile and hopeless labour, rolling a massive rock to the top of a hill in Hades, only to see it roll down again, requiring his task to be endlessly repeated. Camus takes this ancient myth and through the recognition of the pointlessness of his existence, affords a moment of insight to Sisyphus.

> That hour like a breathing-space which returns as surely as his suffering, that is the hour of consciousness. At each of those moments when he leaves the heights and gradually sinks towards the lairs of the gods, he is superior to his fate. He is stronger than his rock ... The workman of today works every day in his life at the same tasks and his fate is no less absurd. But it is tragic only at the rare moments when it becomes conscious[1].

The upheavals of the early twentieth century in Europe brought

1. Albert Camus. *Le Mythe de Sisyphe.* trans. O'Brien, J. Hamilton, 1955. It is not entirely clear why Sisyphus has been condemned to this endless task, but it would appear that he was guilty of a certain degree of levity in his relationship with the gods. Camus offers a number of reasons, all of them appropriate to the existential mid-twentieth-century mind.

about a sense of metaphysical loss articulated by existentialism. Eugène Ionesco saw the modern condition as being one cut off from metaphysical and transcendental roots. Equally we may recall the lines of Yeats in *The Second Coming*, 'The centre cannot hold, mere anarchy is loosed upon the world'. The theatrical forms that emerged and related to existentialism are commonly referred to, somewhat simplistically as the *The Theatre of the Absurd*. The title was in fact one imposed by the journalistic critic, Martin Esslin, in his book of that title. Although, what we may refer to legitimately as an ideological genre related to concepts of Hegelian idealism, theatre that sought either to mourn the loss of a metaphysical centre to human existence in post-war Europe, and theatre that sought some kind of (secular) spiritual renewal through idealist forms of theatre, while finding its adherents in the rest of continental Europe, never sat easily within the English mind. The two playwrights most prominent in this field are obviously Samuel Beckett and Harold Pinter, neither of whom quite fit into that sense of metaphysics as represented by many continental European contemporaries. Beckett was, of course, an Irishman who wrote mainly in French, and his work does have that sense of the existential view, the *via negativa*, and also retains much that may be discerned as local and Irish whimsy. Harold Pinter, even in his early work, managed to translate the metaphysical sensibility into a very English, psychologically concrete world, inhabited not by lost souls, but by familiar people whose sense of dislocation was rooted in pictures of the 'real' world of English urban everyday life.

A good example of the problems of translating Continental absurd metaphysics into England was the celebrated ideological battle between Eugène Ionesco and Kenneth Tynan. Tynan was the theatre critic for *The Observer*, who in the 1950s and 1960s was regarded generally as the *enfant terrible* of the radical theatre critics (although his radicalism was more to do with his individualistic liberalism than it was with socialism). Tynan, in response to productions of Ionesco's plays, *The Lesson* and *The Chairs*, took his stand by the theatre of social values. He attacked Ionesco thus:

> Ionesco's is a world of isolated robots, conversing in cartoon-strip balloons of dialogue that are sometimes hilarious, sometimes evocative, and quite often neither, on which occasions they become profoundly tiresome.

Ionesco exercised the right to reply in the newspaper for which Tynan worked:

> An ideological play can be no more than the vulgarisation of an ideology. In my view, a work of art has its own means of directly apprehending the real ... I think that writers like Sartre, Osborne, Miller, Brecht etc., are simply the new *auteurs du boulevard*, representatives of a left-wing conformism which is just as lamentable as the right-wing sort. These writers offer nothing that one does not know already, through books and political speeches.

Ionesco's claim to be apolitical is that of many idealist artists, wherein they see their work as being transcendent of ideology and history.

Structuralism

In the 1960s there emerged in Europe a movement that in some senses was purely philosophical, and in other senses was more a critical practice. The general heading under which the movement may be classified is structuralism. Any attempt to explain structuralism in a singular sense, would fail to understand the complexity of a theoretical and critical system that draws on the materialism of Marx, while acknowledging its debt to the anthropologist, Levi Strauss. In many ways Levi Strauss was the starting point for structuralism, in which one of its basic premises maintained that humanity's choices were determined by the existing physical, social and cultural determinants that formed the basic units of our consciousness. This shows structuralism as opposed to existentialism, which in its non-marxian interpretation, saw human beings as more or less free agents[2].

Levi Strauss held the view that, through their systems of mythology, we may argue that all societies possess similar underlying psychological structures. Although no real progress was made from Strauss' position he did influence the thinking of the psychologist Louis Lacan and the Marxist Louis Althusser in their different searches for underlying structures. For Lacan the key lay in perceiving the unconscious as a text and therefore meaning may lie in the individual's use of language. Althusser, while denying the structuralist label, did attempt to analyse underlying economic and class structures in the societies that he studied.

Certainly the most significant studies that emerged from structuralist thought were prosecuted by the scholars who were at the forefront of the developing science of linguistics. Building on the work of Ferdinand de Saussure were the post-war linguistic structuralists Roland Barthes and Noam Chomsky, who posited the idea that language is composed of elements that logically relate to each other. Since this relationship orders one's thoughts and therefore determines one's ideas, what one says or writes determines what one thinks rather than the opposite. Certainly one might hazard a structuralist analogy in the theatre by arguing that it is the economic and architectural space of theatre that determines the dramatic structure of a play, rather than the other way around. Without a doubt the conditions of production in the late sixteenth-century theatre of London are analogous in this sense.

While many structuralists would either deny or ignore such a practical and historically orientated analogy, the intellectuals who have retreated from structuralism, have done so because they reacted against what they perceived to be an imposition of a deterministic order on reality. This is a manifestation of determinism, whether historical or linguistic, or indeed a conjunction of the two, that subverts both the metaphysical and the existential construction of reality[3].

2. For a Marxist development of existentialism, see the later work of Jean-Paul Sartre. If existentialism is given meaning through chosen commitment, then for Sartre, the commitment was to communism, for example Nakrassov.

3. We must take into account the argument that prosecutes the case that the concepts of the metaphysical and the existential are not necessarily in a binary opposition.

Poststructuralism

It was inevitable that structuralism itself should come under scrutiny. Certainly in the 1970s and 1980s in Europe, cultural analysis has undertaken a direction that is termed either poststructuralism or post-modernism. Certainly the latter title is the more appropriate one, if we consider structuralism as a part of European modernism. Philosophers of language such as Jacques Derrida, Roland Barthes and Michel Foucault have all denied the universal, timeless mental structures sought after by Levi Strauss (which of course could equally be associated with aspects of liberal humanistic thought emanating from nineteenth-century critics such as Matthew Arnold), contending that thought patterns change over time. Foucault, in particular, was at pains to deny that he was a structuralist, refuting the idea of universal truths, his practice was to historicise 'grand abstractions'. His discourses on historical and institutional contexts have proved appealing to critics and artists on the intellectual left, but his focus on power struggle as the ultimate determinant has not proved conducive to progressive radical philosophies.

Foucault apart, post-modernism in its deconstruction of accepted concepts of hermeneutically sealed texts and the opening and fragmentation of culture to a general science of signs, referred to as semiotics, has led to a general denial of history as progression. The argument that everything from poetry to telephone directories (in the linguistic vocabulary) and the range of visual imagery foregrounded in Europe, by the rapid development of film and television as primary areas of signification in our everyday lives, has challenged certain types of historically based scholarship; primarily those that focus on a 'great tradition' of European culture. Post-modernism has typically ventured into a critique of not only language, but also history, truth, time, space, and existence. The 'end of history' is becoming a popular calling signal to art that can only feed upon past imagery to create intertextual collages. Art, it is argued, can only talk to itself. With the 'end of history' comes the end of procreation; all that is left is masturbation. The images of art, in their excess of signification, talk only to themselves. This requires, as Umberto Eco has argued, a finely tuned audience that is capable of detecting the intertextual references, and by so doing, constructing an ever self-regenerating and self-referential poetics[4].

Marxism

In some senses, we may argue that a materialist poetics of twentieth-century theatre had its intellectual genesis in the nineteenth century, with the publication of *The German Ideology* (1846)[5]. Undoubtedly Marxism has had a deep and lasting part to play in the development of theatre in Europe throughout the twentieth century. If an idealist ideological line stretches back to Hegel, and even to the English Romantics and has found its apotheosis in existentialism, or such figures as Antonin Artaud, Jerzy Grotowski and Peter Brook, then a

4. Umberto Eco, 'Casablanca: cult movies and intertextual collage' in *Faith in Fakes*. London: Martin Secker and Warburg Ltd. 1986.

5. Karl Marx and Friedrich Engels, *The German Ideology*. trans. and ed. S Ryazanskaya. London: Lawrence and Wishart. 1965.

materialist ideological line reaches from Marx through to Bertolt Brecht, Erwin Piscator, John McGrath and the whole wave of post-war British left-wing 'Fringe' theatre. Arguably, the ideas and practices of Bertolt Brecht have had more influence on post-war British theatre, than anyone else in Europe.

What has emerged in post-war Europe has not been the totalitarian form of Marxism that was imposed by Stalin in the Soviet Union. The invasion of Hungary in 1956, by the Soviet forces and the increasingly oppressive and totalitarian face of communism in what became known as the Eastern Bloc, alienated many people on the political left in Western Europe. After such an intellectual fragmentation, what was espoused, and has had its subsequent influence, has been the liberating and emancipatory form of Marxism. The 'new' thought has owed much to the Frankfurt School of Theodor Adorno and Herbert Marcuse (not forgetting Walter Benjamin on the fringes of the Frankfurt School) and in Italy, Antonio Gramsci.

Adorno's work on the function of art has, along with Brecht, Benjamin and Gramsci, made a significant contribution to developments in theatre in Europe, particularly in the last twenty years in relation to certain aspects of post-modernism. Adorno believed that the products of artists throughout the history of Europe from the Medieval period, through the Renaissance to the present day, had preserved a degree of autonomy from the purely pragmatic interests of a culture's economic needs. Similarly, Gramsci argued against the classic Marxist over-simple base and superstructural relationship between ideology and economic structure, focusing on the potentiality for ideologies to reproduce themselves and to 'mutate' without direct reference to the base structure.

Adorno referred to 'autonomous' art, meaning that art had the potentiality to represent individual experiences in such a way as to illuminate their meaning. This may mean that images of beauty and order, or contradiction and dissonance, are produced often simultaneously, both leaving and highlighting perceptions of reality. The objects of art may be drawn from the established hegemonic conventions, but the conventions of order may be portrayed in a non-conventional manner. Of course this is very close to the basic premise contained in Bertolt Brecht's arguments about the function of art. Brecht wished to construct a form of theatre that would allow the contradictions in our view of reality to be exposed. As opposed to an ideology of art that presents the art object (performance of a play, a painting and so on) as a social totality. Brecht's observation may serve as a simple example: art that allows us to see our mothers as our father's lover. As such, art has the potential to be subversive. Its potentiality for 'truth' lies in its capacity to allow the audience the opportunity to restructure conventional patterns of meaning.

Where thinkers like Adorno have been appropriated as a focus of interest to many contemporary postmodern European theatre workers, Brecht has been seen as belonging to the modernist era.

Brecht, it is argued is still represented by a fixed dramatic text that, in spite of the possible radicalism of his original context of experimentation, is now locked into a theatrical canon that is simultaneously appropriated and rejected by bourgeois culture. Traditionally, it is argued, most political theatre of the early twentieth century has drawn upon the conventions established by the modernist epic paradigm. For the postmodern critique this implies a dialectical structure that offers the audience only a binary choice of reading positions. The spectator is steered to the closure of a synthesis arising from a clash of grand narratives.

The focus interest among many materialist theatre workers is on the potentiality of theatre to reveal the construction of the theatrical and cultural discourses that shape the performance, so as to undermine its own claims to truth. Confining Brecht to a binary dialectic of the so-called brechtian structure, is itself already a product of cultural determinants.

It would be inaccurate to class Adorno, or any of the Frankfurt school in the areas of the postmodern thought (and inaction!). What Adorno does offer, is the opportunity for culture to be seen as a complex issue that cannot be bound by the classic Marxist base/superstructure model, which in its own time led to the constraints of 'socialist realism', with art serving the needs of the party, to arise under Stalin.

Theatre Practitioners in Europe: 1957–1973

The dates of this first section dealing with the work of specific European theatre practitioners, indicate the year of the signing of the Treaty of Rome to the entry of the United Kingdom into what was then the single Europe Act of 1973.

The essays in this group will comprise, as an overview, commentaries on the work of a wide (but not all inclusive) range of theatre practitioners. The material is organised in such a way as to enable the reader to see the particular theatre practitioner in a European and historical context and to, in some ways, relate that practitioner to the broader philosophical questions that have already been addressed. Some of the individuals will be a part of mainstream theatrical conventions, belonging to large subsidised companies, or to well known commercial theatres. Other people will be known more for their individual enterprise, or for the subversive and fringe nature of their work. The term 'fringe' is also to be addressed; predominantly coming from the British theatre of the 1960s, 1970s and 1980s, it is a term that may be usefully employed when articulating the role played by such people as Dario Fo.

Certainly a notable factor in the rebuilding of European theatre after the Second World War, was the desire to re-establish the sense of a country's culture; culture in the evaluative, rather than the analytic sense. In the case of countries that had been physically occupied and devastated, there was the need for a tangible and concrete sense of themselves as a part of European heritage. This may appear to be a direct contradiction of the preoccupations addressed in the introduction to this volume. However, it is arguably the very way by which the complexities (and contradictions) are revealed. The preoccupations with the uncertainty of human progress often provide the fuel by which culture(s) may be developed or re-invented.

It is therefore no accident that when we look at what was after the Second World War, the Federal Republic of Germany, we see a rapid and extensive theatre building and refurbishment programme. From 1948 (with the reform of the German currency) over 200 theatres were repaired, renovated, extended, or built from scratch. By 1972, there were in 77 towns and cities in West Germany and West Berlin, 86 publicly controlled theatre institutions with 192 halls between them, including those for opera and ballet. There were also 78 private theatres, most of which received smaller contributions from public funds[1].

The London exhibition of post-war German theatre architecture in 1968 was impressive. It sent a clear statement to those who

1. Deutscher Bühnenverein, *Theater Statistik* 1971-72. Cologne. 1973.

witnessed the efforts put into this form of cultural identity, that the Germans took theatre and opera more seriously than the British. However, to attempt to build a clear picture, we must take into account two factors. The rebuilding of West Germany after the Second World war was of paramount importance to the Western power block, and although the funds that allowed such a progress were undoubtedly a part of the German economic miracle, the support of the USA cannot be discounted (as of course the German Democratic Republic was supported by the Soviet Union). Equally, regional rivalry in Germany, as a cultural echo of the times before German unification in the nineteenth century, played a not insignificant part in the determination on the part of local, as well as national, authorities to display the resistance of German cultural identity.

The post-war years in European theatre have been marked by the pre-eminence attained by the figure of the director as *auteur*[2]. Although in recent years the status as *auteur* has been challenged by, particularly in Britain, a sense of the collective nature of theatre-making, we would be negligent if we did not give due recognition to the significance of this role in European theatre.

Peter Stein

Peter Stein was born in Berlin in 1937, and was thus well placed to play a part in the complex cultural politics of West Germany's identity in the new Europe. His higher education was in literature and fine art with no formal education in the theatre. In this, he shares a common background with many prominent British post-war directors. His early work, certainly before he joined the West Berlin Schaubühne theatre, was marked by his evident left-wing ideology. Inevitably this espousal of socialism in his work created an uneasy tension between Stein and the authorities, both local and national, in a country that was seen by the West as the bulwark against communism. However, from around 1972 onwards, it appeared to his critics that he was becoming more concerned with what Michael Patterson has referred to as a form of 'aesthetic onanism'; concentrating his direction on the bourgeois tradition, in particular the nineteenth century and abandoning his progressive political focus[3].

Stein's first independent production was *Saved* by the British playwright Edward Bond in 1967. This was followed in 1968 by a production of Bertolt Brecht's play *The Jungle of the Cities*. The production of a play by the leading playwright of communist East Germany has been a fairly contentious issue, but Stein followed this with a production in July of the same year of Peter Weiss's play *Vietnam Discourse*. The production ran for only three nights. The topical nature of what was, to an extent, a piece of *agit-prop* theatre[4] concerning matters of imperialist aggression on the part of the USA in Vietnam. Stein was fully aware of the potential ineffectiveness of political theatre presented in safe middle-class theatres and in an

2. In German and French the accepted title is *Regisseur*.
3. Patterson, M. *Peter Stein: Germany's Leading Theatre Director*. Cambridge: Cambridge University Press. 1981.
4. Agit-Prop or Agitation and Propaganda. The term used to describe theatre pieces devised to ferment political action (agitation) and propaganda.

attempt to constructively subvert his own project, had scrawled across the back wall of stage, the legend 'Documentary Theatre is Crap'. To follow the performance a collection in aid of the National Liberation Front was to have been made, but the collection was prohibited and Stein's contract not renewed.

The timing of this element of political activity in the German theatre is notable, largely because of the political events happening in France during the summer of 1968. This was the summer of the student and worker action on the streets of Paris. The Left-wing political activity was an immediate and practical action arising from the 'new' Marxism evolving from the Frankfurt school and associated political thinkers and activists such as Antonio Gramsci. The course taken by Europe at this time may have been, with the American involvement in Vietnam serving as a focus, very different from the one that it actually took.

Peter Stein was appointed Director of the West Berlin Schaubühne theatre in 1970. The Schaubühne was created in 1962 by students whose main concern was to create a theatre practice that rejected the hierarchical structures of both the municipal subsidised theatres and the commercially run theatres. Stein's reputation for thorough research and collective practice made him a seemingly ideal choice to head this 'alternative' theatre. It would seem that in this context, the theatre appropriate to the new thought among students and intellectuals in the Europe of the late 1960s, might find realisation. A combination of the right-wing reaction of the 1970s and the compromises made by the Schaubühne resulted in, what is now from the perspective of the 1990s, an all too familiar pragmatism. Stein himself said that:

> The decision to direct a certain play does not follow any ideological or aesthetic programme, but results from impulses of a given situation.

Perhaps the exemplifier for this change of ideological direction was Stein's production of Shakespeare's play, *As You Like It*. His methodology was a familiar one to those who knew his work: many weeks (sometimes even months) of research and rehearsal with the actors and designers. Out of this research came a working of the text that would, to the eyes of many British critics seem an impertinence. Stein often worked with sets that enabled him to stage related scenes simultaneously, or to reveal characters as they were, simultaneously with how they are now. The setting for *As You Like It* was housed in a huge film studio, in which the scenes in Duke Frederick's court were played out in one place, coldly lit and coloured, with isolated figures moving on raised catwalks. The audience were then required to move into another immense space and found themselves physically in the midst of the Forest of Arden. The reworking of the text, juxtaposing scenes in various ways and reordering or repeating scenes is a technique familiar to the continental European eye, as we will see when we look at the work of Giorgio Strehler. However the British, as it is with many aspects of their view of Europeanism, seem to operate by less flexible ideological constructs. Perhaps one distinct difference is the space afforded by the British to the pre-eminence of the literary text as a fixed entity. Whereas many of the other European cultures are serious about theatre as a form in its own right, allowing the theatrical reading to roam freely, unrestrained by a valorised sense of the text's meaning. Stein's deliberate juxtaposing of time sequences, encouraging the audience to see time as fragmented, rather than as a linear progression, seems to bear out many of the preoccupations in European thought that have already been delineated.

Peter Weiss

Much of what may be said about the period of European cultural history from 1957 to 1974, as we have seen with the work of Peter Stein, hinges around the reactions to Marxism provoked by the reaction against Soviet communism/Stalinism, as the intellectuals in the West learned of the repressions culminating in the atrocities against Hungary in 1956. The rethinking of left-wing political philosophy, led by the Frankfurt School, produced a generation in the theatre that rejected the seeming modernism of absurdism and surrealism and the quasi-religiosity of Artaud. One of the early notorious successes of Peter Stein was his production of Peter Weiss' play *Vietnam Discourses*. The full title is typically revealing:

> *Discourse concerning the Origin and Course of the Prolonged War of Liberation in Vietnam as an Example of the Need of the Oppressed to Take up Arms against their Oppressors as well as as the Attempt by the United States of America to Destroy the Basis of the Revolution.*

Weiss rejected the retreat, made by many writers, into a 'non-political' subjective response to the world of the late twentieth century. Particularly in the German Federal Republic, the reaction to the recent Nazi past was to attempt to espouse a non- politically aligned position. This generated a complex ideological patterning in the post-war culture of western Germany. There was, without doubt, political alignment in that West Germany was a part of the Western Bloc under the influence of the United States of America. However, equally there was the impetus towards an individualistic ideology, that allowed operation within the national hegemonic complexity that evolved out of the ruins of war; hence the articulating of the experience of the world in the subjective, seemingly uncommitted, language of many post-war theatrically closed cultures.

In the West, what emerged as opposition to the closed subjective ideology, was an alternative to the close adherence to the 'party line', demanded by Stalinism and for that matter Nazism; both of which required, respectively, their own versions of 'socialist realism' whereby art serves the needs of the party. The belief was that political intent does not imply a close adherence to a party line. The purpose of art, if we are to refer again to Brecht and Benjamin, is to disrupt an accepted view of reality. The idea of documentary theatre emerged as a form having the potential to offer a sense of authenticity in the narrative presented to an audience. This does not necessarily imply the factual agit-prop style of *The Living Newspaper*, but offers an open-ended cultural experience, where the aim is to enable the members of an audience to observe the dialectical process and to make their own decisions regarding the perspectives of reality offered by the range of theatrical narratives.

Thus, we may observe a movement away from Weiss' post-war identity as a rootless *emigré*, with largely unsuccessful work, displaying a tendency towards the Kafkaesque and a form of self-discovery[5]. When Weiss was in his late forties, he produced the first of the new style documentary works which were to prove interesting, not only in their intrinsic merits, but also in the manner by which they were appropriated by differing ideological interests. The first of these 'documentaries' was produced in 1964, with almost as long a title as the later *Vietnam Discourses*:

> *The Persecution and Assassination of Jean-Paul Marat as Performed by the Inmates of the Asylum of Charenton under the Direction of the Marquis de Sade.*

The *Marat Sade* as it is popularly known, represents well the complex ideological positions of artists, particularly Germans, at this point in European history. The play itself could be said to represent three readings of both social culture and the stage. Set in what is referred to as a lunatic asylum, the play shows the Marquis de Sade supervising a performance by patients of the murder of Marat. Marat's position is that of the revolutionary; the figure conscious of ideology and the need for revolution. The Marquis de Sade is the intellectual individualist; the proto-bourgeois (despite his aristocratic position) who is only able to view the world in terms of the individual. The play itself is both product of and commentary upon the cultural context of its making.

It is apposite to this argument, to note three theatrical readings of the play: the West Berlin premiere, Peter Brooks's London production of 1965 and the East German production later in that year. Strictly speaking, the two latter examples should be outside of the remit of this research, as neither were members of the European Community at this time. However, the point to be made is germane to the argument, relating as it is, to the cultural context of post-war Europe. In West Berlin, it would come as no great surprise that the over-lying theme focused on the need for compromise, recognising the need to avoid, at all costs, the dangers of dictatorship from the left or the right. While Brook, in London in the mid-1960s, took an approach that emphasised the extreme individualism of de Sade's position, drawing on the influence of Antonin Artaud and his concept of 'theatre of cruelty', meaning the harsh awakening of the senses of both the audience and the performers. Inevitably, the East

5. Weiss lived in England, Czechoslovakia, Switzerland and Sweden.

Berlin reading articulated the accuracy of Marat's argument as the
revolutionary, while ignoring the very real irony of performing this
reading in the light of the realities of Stalinist repression in East
Germany.

Given the argument that a single text may well have the potential
for an infinite plurality of meaning, it is necessary to take note of the
contexts for the production of those meanings. The position of
Western Europe at this particular point in Europe's history, was
complex to say the least. If we care to see it in a particular way, the
multi-layered meanings of Weiss' play the *Marat Sade*, may operate as
cultural paradigms for the complex ideological discourses of Europe
that emerge in the attempt to create a coherent identity.

While the *Marat Sade* offered the possibility of a subtle and
complex debate on the question of personal and political identity in
post war Europe, his later play of 1968 dealt more obviously with
what we may term the 'Theatre of Fact'. At this point the debt to the
American *Living Newspaper*[6] and Erwin Piscator becomes clear.
Vietnam Discourses, which dealt with the 2,500 year long Vietnamese
struggle for liberation, offered a collage of documentary images
juxtaposed with narratives taken from history and contemporary
experience, but in terms of the theatre event, fictionalised. This
technique developed in the *Living Newspaper*, often created its
narrative by demonstrating the effect of broad historical events on
the personal lives of fictional characters. The influence of this
convention is clearly seen in Clifford Odets' play, *Waiting For Lefty*.
Though not a part of the *Living Newspaper* project, Odets took the
theme of a particular taxi drivers' strike in the American depression;
using the frame of a union meeting, he demonstrated the effects of
deprivation on the personal lives of individuals. In many ways this
preceded the popular contemporary call of 'personal is political'.
Vietnam Discourses fitted well into the debates in Europe in the late
1960s. It dealt with Europe's relationships with the United States of
America and that country's involvement with Vietnam, and it created
a furore that, among other consequences, led to the banning of Peter
Stein's production in Munich.

Weiss was never an easy playwright to pin down to a specific
ideological position. His perceptions, as well as his forms of work,
constantly changed. A later play, *Hölderlin*, seems to hark back almost
to a Hegelian idea that outward material condition is not always
commensurate with the 'spiritual' condition. Although Hegel's
argument was perhaps more to do with material deprivation not
being able to affect a sense of spiritual freedom, the analogy is close
to *Hölderlin*. The revolutionary poet in exile (as Weiss had been in
Sweden) is condemned by everyone to be insane; a topic also dealt
with by Weiss in 1970, in his play *Trotsky in Exile*. The theme deals
with the argument that the great figures of the nineteenth century
had made compromises with their material conditions and the
question is asked, is this the inevitable reality that all revolutionaries
must face? It would seem that Weiss has pre-empted the cynical

6. The *Living Newspaper*,
    the documentary,
    newsreel-like
    presentation of current
    events, has been used
    in agitational theatre
    in many countries, but
    its flowering in the
    West was undoubtedly
    the American *Living
    Newspaper* created by
    Elmer Rice and the
    Federal Theatre Project in
    1935.

mood of the 1970s in Europe; after the revolutions of the 1960s, the revisions of the 1970s.

Peter Handke

The generation following Weiss, was that of Peter Handke, who in particular seems to articulate in theatrical form aspects of the linguistic debates of structuralist theory. Strictly speaking, Handke should not be included in this volume, as he is Austrian and not at this point in history a part of what we are identifying as the European Community; nevertheless, his presence should not be ignored. That he is a writer in the German language brings him close to the argument at this point, but he may also serve as a sideways comment on the development of this aspect of European identity.

Handke's main theme may be said to be the (European) crisis of language. In a brief examination of his play *Kasper* (1969), Handke takes the well known story of Kaspar Hauser, who lived in total isolation without human speech until adulthood. Handke builds that narrative into a discourse on the concept that language, while defining us, encloses us in patterns of hegemonic convention. His predominant source was Wittgenstein and 'the reflection of language', but he took these forms of linguistic argument to the point where he was no longer concerned with an attempted objective reality, but only concerned with the reality of the words themselves.

Glancing back to Handke's first notable play *Offending the Audience* (1966), we see a *sprechstuck* of four speakers who, over the period of about an hour, verbally abuse the audience, while constantly contradicting themselves and subverting any possible responses from the audience; they aim to expose the manipulative effects of language. Further forward to 1969 with his play *My Foot My Tutor*, we observe that language stops altogether. The authority that the players take unto themselves, as do all performers once the audience is seated and bound to them, becomes more terrifying in this mute performance.

Handke's concerns with a distrust of acceptance of a concept of objective reality may not ultimately be at one with the central discourses of structuralist linguistic theory, but nor is it entirely removed. Again theatre reveals its potentiality as a cultural site, whereby contemporary theories of language and identity are given, at the least, a concrete form of interaction between what we may think of as the self and its relationship with the other: performer(s) and audience.

Günter Grass

A leading member of the *Gruppe 47* (as was Handke) Günter Grass has been in the mainstream of West Germany's search for its post-war identity. Possibly better known as a novelist, he has experimented with most of the later twentieth-century genres of playwriting, achieving wide spread recognition with his play, *The Plebians*

Rehearse The Uprising. This play, which draws on Shakespeare's *Coriolanus* and a supposed rehearsal by Brecht for his version of that play, represents again, one of the many debates questioning the identity of self and the complex problem of how political art functions in relation to the reality of a particular context.

The play is set in the Berliner Ensemble on June 17 1953, when East German workers demonstrated against government demands for higher productivity. The figure of Bertolt Brecht is depicted in a character referred to only as the Boss, who at the time of the workers' demonstrations, is in rehearsal for a production of *Coriolanus*. The workers ask for the Boss's support, which he refuses to give, but at the same time refusing to denounce the demonstrations when asked to do so by the Stalinist authorities.

It is worthwhile spending a little time outlining the nature of these demonstrations, for they were not simply related to wage demands (although that voice can never be separated from broader political issues). The initial action on the part of the Stalinist government was referred to on June 14 by the Central Organ of the Socialist Unity Party, *Neues Deutschland*, as 'sledge hammer' techniques that denied any democratic voice to the workers. A general strike was called for June 17 and workers were asked to attend a rally on Strausberger Platz that morning. The day before a group of workers had gone to 'Radio in the American Sector' (R.I.A.S) and appealed for their support. The outcome was that a resolution listing their demands was broadcast on June 18. How far the motives of the American sector radio were objective we probably shall never know, but nevertheless, the resolutions broadcast make clear that the level of dissatisfaction was profound and far reaching:

- payment of wages in accordance with the old norms on the next pay day;
- immediate reduction in the cost of living;
- free and secretive elections;
- no punitive measures against strikers and their spokesmen.

One can never be sure what position the governments in western Europe were taking at this point, but the issue is important, if only to illuminate the ideological dilemmas facing the left in the West, when confronted by the authoritarian position taken by the Soviet bloc.

Günter Grass' position in the play is certainly more complex than a simple direct attack on what one might suppose to be Brecht's complicity with the East German government. In the play the Boss (Brecht), in refusing to give his public support for the demonstration (which is in its early stages), argues that unplanned action is senseless. He continues with his rehearsal, incorporating the real workers, in order to observe their reactions to issues dealt with in his attempt to politicise Shakespeare's play for the twentieth century.

The position of Grass is a curious and complex one. In some ways he is seemingly post-modern, in his conscious (and some might say cynical) exploitation of various aspects of Brecht's dramaturgy and techniques, while clearly not entirely at one with their original political points. This may clearly be seen in much of his early work, where he uses deliberate pastiche, in first an expressionist style, and then later in a series of 'absurd' plays. The earlier work concentrates on exposing the grotesqueness of the Nazi period, while the experiments with the absurd genre are more to do with contemporary 1960 political corruption and coercion. The culmination of the appropriations is to be found in *Plebians Rehearse The Uprising.*

Jean-Louis Barrault

Turning from Germany to France, the figure of Jean-Louis Barrault features significantly in this period of European development (1957-1974). I do not mean in any sense to isolate the individual as a cultural icon, but as an expression of a particular instance of cultural liberalism, that found itself uneasy with the materialist debates that were so prevalent in the 1960s.

Barrault had been a significant figure in the French theatre for many years as actor, producer, director and adapter since his early work in the 1930s, when he was hailed by the French visionary, Antonin Artaud, as having achieved his own ideal in the theatre[7]. Barrault is probably best known outside France for his role as Baptiste in the film, *Les Enfants du Paradis.* His professional associates represent many notable figures within pre- and post-war French theatre, including Charles Dullin, André Gide, Jean-Paul Sartre and Paul Claudel. Likewise his craft includes mime as well as acting and directing. Well known abroad, especially in Britain, Barrault was applauded for his innovations as a director with classic texts of Britain and Germany, as well as with the French canon. Equally, his reputation for experimental work with authors such as Ionesco, gave him a reputation as a member of the avant-garde. It is this reputation that provides the cultural location for the interesting ideological clash, into which Barrault was drawn in the Paris political demonstrations of 1968.

His autobiography depicts a man who is totally devoted to his art[8]. This in a sense is the crux of the matter. For Barrault, art is transcendent of other more 'material' matters. This is not to say that his work is ethereal and without the materiality of theatrical craft; quite the reverse, long passages of his books are devoted to the craft of his theatre. The question is more to do with his ideology regarding the function of art. In this he views art as transcendent of cultural materiality. In the liberal humanist tradition, from the early nineteenth century, Barrault sees for art an aesthetic function operating by its own laws. This is made clear in one of the final chapters of the autobiography entitled, *May '68, Collective Ordeal, Individual Ordeal.*

This chapter is an account of how Barrault's theatre company, *Théâtre des Nations,* was taken over by the student demonstrators. An event which laid bare the conflict between the sensibilities of the

7. Artaud's ideas are to many people, largely incoherent, but it is generally understood that he sought after a sense of the spiritual in the theatre; a reclaiming of total emotional and physical commitment as a rejection of 'psychologism'.

8. Jean-Louis Barrault. *Memories for Tomorrow: The memoirs of Jean-Louis Barrault.* trans. Griffen, J. London: Thames and Hudson. 1974.

artist against, what Barrault perceived as the cynical philistinism of the revolutionaries. He made it quite clear that he had a liberal sympathy with the idea of protest, but that what was happening in Paris was something alien to his culture.

> The so-called 'May events' still puzzle public opinion. People have had the shock, lived through the fear, imagined the reaction .... It is not a French affair, it is a world-wide phenomenon. In May the lightning struck in Paris. That is all. The storm, it seems to me, came from far away, and is still wandering around the world .... For the second time I had fallen into the trap. I was left with the disagreeable impression of something which I did not understand, but which seemed to me calculated and, here, again, to have come from far away — yes, I repeat, from Far Away[9].

It is difficult not to draw parallels with Margaret Thatcher's pronouncements against 'alien political philosophies in our midst', but probably unfair. Barrault was genuinely shocked by his confrontation with the action of the May demonstrations. He saw a part of himself belonging to what he termed the underground movement. This is demonstrated by the fact that on the eve of the 'invasion' of the Odéon, he had organised an evening of 'beatnik poetry', a term which had long since left popular usage by 1968. What really dismayed his artistic and humanistic sensibility, was the description of his theatre (the performances, not necessarily the building) as 'an emblem of bourgeois culture'. His disorientation at the attempt at popular culture through a popular uprising is perhaps the salient feature. Barrault failed to see that his 'avant-gardism' bore little relationship to a radical concept of the potentiality of popular art. A figure such as Peter Stein may have reached an ideological hiatus by the mid 1970s, but he maintained a sense of contemporary European thought, that Barrault's essentially nineteenth-century liberal humanism, never understood.

Out of the confusion of the May days at the Odéon, Barrault articulated four points that he understood were the demands of the occupiers of his theatre:

1. that the action of the students was not directed against either a man or a programme (this was soon stated in their first *bulletin d'occupation*);
2. that the *Théâtre de France*, as an emblem of 'bourgeois culture' was suppressed;
3. that the Odéon would now be used as a political form;
4. that no dialogue (discussion) was possible[10].

Barrault saw the events becoming more and more anarchic, as he perceived fewer and fewer students involved in the occupation of the Odéon and more, what he terms in his autobiography as, 'agitators and bruisers of all sorts'. If Barrault had a liberal sympathy with certain student grievances, he also believed in the necessity of rescuing art from politics. His quotation of Pascal would seem to

9. *Ibid.* pp.311–313.
10. *Ibid.* pp.314–315.

sum up his position. 'When Plato and Aristotle wrote about politics, it was as if they had to run a madhouse'[11].

Roger Planchon

On April 8 1959, André Malraux as Minister of state for Cultural Affairs, announced a programme to revitalise the French national theatres. The reform was essentially one of restructuring and redistribution of repertory resources. There had, for some years been a degree of dissatisfaction with the recent history of the *Comédie Française*. Under the new plan, Claude Bréart de Boisanger was appointed director of the *Comédie Française*, which was then deprived of one of its two subsidiary theatres. One of them, the *Salle Luxembourg*, was now to be operated by Jean Louis Barrault and renamed the *Théâtre de France*. The broader implications were to do with a widening of the scope of the funding for theatre in France, moving away from the old High Art ideals of French nineteenth-century cultural hegemony, towards an egalitarianism more appropriate to the new Europe.

Roger Planchon was one director who seems to have been a part of this new egalitarian policy, offering a rather different perspective on the function of theatre in France in the 1960s, to that embodied by Barrault. While Barrault experimented with the avant-garde, but nevertheless appealed to the *cognoscenti*, Planchon was more concerned with the broad functional appeal of his theatre. This example is not an argument for a binary polarisation of ideology in French theatre at this time; the situation is more complex than that. However, this context does point to the difficulty involved in identifying the exact nature of cultural operations in the theatre. Barrault's, or for that matter anybody's avant-gardism, does not necessarily imply popular art in the radical leftist sense. This argument will be made clear perhaps when after 1974, we deal with liberal and leftist theatre in Britain after joining the EEC. The pertinent case would be in the work of Peter Brook, whose experiments in theatre, it may be argued, are a curious mix of the avant-garde and post-colonialism.

Planchon's working class origins serve rather more than a spurious and nostalgic explanation for the nature of his work in French theatre. He was largely self educated, with the result that he was less than hampered by the restrictions that a formal education can sometimes place upon the individual. His very clear and simple aim was, and is, to bring a popular theatre to as broad an audience as possible. As his work developed through the 1950s and into the 1960s, it is possible to detect a more clearly formulated and articulated political theory informing his theatre practice. Certainly ·by the time of the late 1960s, the time of politics moving out on to the streets, Planchon committed himself to an anti-establishment declaration commenting on the work of the managers of most of France's subsidised theatres.

After starting work in the early 1950s, Planchon experimented

11. *Ibid.* p.319.

with an eclectic range of styles; moving easily between the avant-garde plays of Adamov and Ionesco, to self-scripted musical comedies. He did this with his amateur group, which turned professional after winning a prize in a competition in Lyon. In this period Planchon was experimenting with, and learning about, a wide range of theatrical styles. His interests included English, Elizabethan stagecraft and American gangster films among other sources for his growing resource. This electism could start to sound like the so many disparate images produced by a devotee of post-modernism, the rationale being that there are no more new stories, so we now only revel in the intertextuality produced by eclecticism. This would be a cynical, but accurate assessment, if it were not for the influence of Jean Vilar and Bertolt Brecht. Vilar is perhaps best known for his directorship of the *Théâtre National Populaire* at Chaillot, where his aim was to produce a theatre as popular and as 'classless' as was possible. His insistence was that theatre should be a service available to all, just as water or electricity. Such an ideal sounds hollow today when not only is theatre having to become more and more commercial in its dealings, but the basic services in the UK are now privatised.

Vilar's exemplar was reinforced by a meeting with Bertolt Brecht in 1954. It was through this meeting, and to an extent the influence of Adamov, that Planchon was able to develop a theoretical Marxist base to his popular theatrical stagecraft. He became one of France's foremost director's of the plays of Brecht, offering not a cautious and reverential rendering of the literary text, but a complex and thoroughly theatrical text in its own right. Here we see one of the fundamental distinctions between much of what was being developed on the continental mainland, and what has evolved in Britain.

Planchon serves well as an example of this very fundamental distinction, between the British and the continental European attitude towards the text and the performance. Planchon coined a term *écriture scènique* which may be translated as 'scenic writing', in order to express the importance of the director's role in the creation of the theatrical performance. His view was that the director, rather than simply serving what are determined as the needs of the text (that is being subordinate to the text) should be seen to complement the role of the author of the text. His term then, for the author's role, was that of dramatic writing. Scenic writing and dramatic writing should be seen as equal and complementary roles within the theatrical process. This concept sits uneasily in the British mind, where for so long the play, as literary object, has been held to be culturally pre-eminent over the theatrical performance.

To digress momentarily from Planchon's work, it is worth examining a little further the idea of the director that is prevalent in Germany and Italy, as well as France. They look upon the director as the primary creator of the production. The practice that brings together the visual and aural imagery of a play is taken as a serious language in its own right; the play as literary text therefore becoming one of the factors (as opposed to the single prime factor) in the performative practice. Edward Gordon Craig saw the theatre as the art of the designer and the director; the actor being relegated to the role of *über marionette*. The technical name in French, for the director, is *metteur-en-scène*, with particular directors held in very high regard being afforded the title of *animateur*. The designation implies s/he who is the unifier of all that is seen and heard on stage.

There is a problem, however, with this designation, especially when, as it was later in his career, afforded to Planchon. While the model of *écriture scènique* combined with dramatic writing is potentially radical and progressive, the structure becomes open to question when it moves towards the idea of *animateur*; certainly if it is conceived of in terms of Craig's model. For Planchon, influenced by Brecht, Vilar and Marxism, the implied autocratic figure of *animateur* seems to be somewhat contradictory. While the contradiction holds true in many cases, Planchon avoided the worst excesses. His work avoided Vilar's concept of theatre as the great unifying force for all society. While his practice drew all the elements of theatrical practice together, it was not to serve a 'master-vision', but to be the result of a collective activity that sought to make the best of theatre available to working class audiences. Equally, his work sought to reveal the injustices in society, rather than appeal to a sense of cultural oneness through art. Much of this work was achieved in the large municipal theatre in the workers' suburb of Lyon that he took over in 1957, when his company achieved the title of *Théâtre National Populaire*.

Aesthetics and Popular Art in Italy
In turning to Italy we may gain another perspective on the cultural patterns evolving in this period of Europe's post-war development, by assaying the work of two quite distinct theatre directors. The work of Giorgio Strehler and Dario Fo represents just such a divergence of the ideology of aesthetics that we have surveyed in France and Germany.

The point to emphasise here is the nature of the role of theatre within the construction of culture, rather than what is often perceived as the isolated actions of individuals. Art is, we may argue, not simply a collection of texts (performances) existing outside the material conditions of economic production; nor is the work of the artist a transcendental vision uninformed by economic laws, obeying only the laws of 'aesthetics'. The production of human consciousness may appear to be governed by laws unrelated to economic production and many students of art are content to believe that it 'exists in a separate realm. However, art is a form of social production and the understanding of this argument can determine our understanding of the nature of art itself. In the work of Strehler and Fo we may be able to observe how the material conditions of their work, form the ideology of their respective aesthetics.

An examination of the work of Giorgio Strehler gives the impression that his theatre is, consciously, politically engaged. In the late 1960s and early 1970s this was apparently so, but only to a limited extent, and may be seen as the general (temporary) shift left-ward in Western Europe, that occurred as a result of the political movements of the late 1960s. Certainly, we may say that on the facts, his work has been, and is, more concerned with contemporary appropriations of European classics, than it ever was with contemporary issues. His 'concept' productions of plays like *The Tempest* were the product of an ideology of individualistic directorial vision, as were those of the more *avant-garde* English directors, rather than an attempt to appropriate the text to a specifically contemporary ideological reading.

This is not to deny that Strehler's individual directorial vision is somehow transcendent of ideology. The question is perhaps more to do with the ideological currency by which we, the potential audience, may be able to locate the director's meaning in the performance. The former will inevitably be what we may express as a closed cultural event; the meaning either being obscure (perhaps even inarticulate, much art hides behind this mask assuming the *masque* of insight). Or the patterning of imagery can only be read by the informed *cognoscenti*, who are in possession of a high degree of information already in their cultural armoury. The latter point offering the potential to appropriate (as one might argue any act of theatrical realisation is an appropriation of the playwright's text) in the sense of popular aesthetics; the performance enabling the audience to confront, through the play, aspects of their own realities. The individualistic vision encloses the theatrical experience to a specific (élite) cultural experience: the popular appropriation opens the event out for debate.

Strehler's main body of work has been with the Piccolo Teatro in Milan, but for a period between 1968 and 1972 he formed the Gruppo Teatro e Azione. This latter venture was directly influenced by the political events in Europe, particularly in Paris. The Piccolo Teatro is a subsidised theatre with the aim of reaching as wide an audience as possible. In many ways its cultural position is very similar to that of the Royal Shakespeare Theatre in the United Kingdom. A curious and complex liberal cultural role is sought by this kind of institution. On the one hand it is confined by the machinery, both economic and architectural, of that kind of liberal bourgeois institution. However, it does have the aspiration of disseminating its culture to as many people as is possible, even though its performances may still be hidebound by a less than popular ideology. In the 1980s his work increasingly became involved with the work of *Théâtre de l'Europe*, for which company he directed the Brecht/Hauptmann play *The Threepenny Opera*.

Strehler's repertoire has been very wide, both internationally and culturally. In the 1950s Brecht was an important influence, but to what extent this betrayed a political affiliation with Brecht, or to what extent Strehler's work was following the kind of appropriation that was undergone in Britain, where the main impetus was to rescue the artist Brecht from his 'repressive' political ideology is difficult to tell. Although his work has covered a very wide range of Italian plays of all periods, his other notable concern has been with Shakespeare, including in his work *Richard III, Julius Caesar* and *Coriolanus*. The Shakespearean production for which he is best known throughout Europe is probably *The Tempest*.

The question of Shakespearean production in post-war Europe is complex, and a distinction needs to be made between the dissemination of this playwright on the English stage and productions in the rest of Europe. It is difficult not to avoid making generalisations, but there is a degree of accuracy in describing the English theatre as being more inclined to foreground the play as literature, than there is to perceive the theatre's potential as a visual medium. The skill of the director, particularly where Shakespeare is concerned, has never, at least by critics, been taken as seriously as that of the poet. In England the cultural construction of Shakespeare over the last 400 years has been such that, not only has he been transformed from theatre maker into the philosopher/prince, but he has been instituted into the central canon of English hegemonic culture. This has meant that the sixteenth-century playwright has become intrinsic to the eternal spirit of England[12].

In the rest of Europe this situation, for obvious reasons, has never been exploited in quite the same way; even considering the place afforded to Shakespeare in the German canon. Strehler is an excellent example by which to understand one of the fundamental differences between the English attitude towards the theatre director, and the position afforded to him or her in the rest of Western Europe.

Strehler's reading of the play, placed the metaphor of theatre itself at the centre of the representation of Prospero. The magical power of Prospero/ Shakespeare/artist is the power of art itself to change the world. To this end the Milan production employed elaborate 'self-reflexive' stage effects in order to facilitate Prospero's objectives in the play's narrative. As an example Ariel, depicted sometimes as a white face clown and at other times as a stage manager, was suspended from the flying space of the stage on what was obviously a theatre cable. There was no attempt to disguise the machinery by which Ariel flew, in fact it became the visible means by which the actor was able to perform, self-consciously, a series of circus acrobatics which could be read as his magic. This is one example of a number of spectacular stage effects employed by Strehler. His aim was, unlike the pictorial spectacles of the late nineteenth-century stage, not to create an illusion but to expose it. Prospero's/Shakespeare's art could enable, but had its limits, and an important point in this production was to expose the limits to which art could be efficacious. Nor must Strehler's exposing of the 'magical' machinery of art be confused with Brecht's concept of *Verfremdung*[13].

12. Examples of nineteenth-century 'deification' of Shakespeare from popular playwright into philosopher/prince may be found in *Shakespeare*. Matthew Arnold. 1844 and *To Shakespeare After Three Hundred Years*. Thomas Hardy. 1926.

13. *Verfremdung*: to induce in the audience a detached and critical stance.

Brecht's exposing of the machinery of theatre was to enable the audience to be reminded that the event was art and not to be absorbed into a belief in the illusion. Thus, being freed from empathy, the audience could read the performance in its relationship to the realities of their histories.

Strehler's treatment of the received Shakespeare text was cavalier, by the values of many English literary scholars. As of course was Peter Stein's production of *As You Like It*. The *masque* scene in *The Tempest* was cut, apparently because it disrupted Strehler's building of the comic scenes and their inspiration from the Italian tradition of *commedie dell' arte*.

Certainly Strehler's production offers a radical challenge to the sanctity of the received literary text. However, its radicalism in a sense is confined in the closed cultural world of self-referential art. In Strehler's work with the Italian canon, there is strong evidence to suggest that he has worked towards a recovery of the Italian *commedia* tradition. However, it maybe argued that this work has been geared towards an appropriation of an Italian popular art form into the enclosed cultural world of 'high art'. In contrast to this impetus, the work on the *commedia* tradition by Dario Fo stands in marked distinction to Strehler's appropriations.

Dario Fo

Dario Fo is a contemporary of Strehler, but works within a very different tradition; in fact very much in the subversive tradition of *commedia dell' arte*.

Fo's work has not been in any sense dedicated to 'reviving' the *commedia dell' arte* as an historical entity, but has more accurately been centred in a similar satiric and anarchic mode that is of the twentieth century[14]. His career has varied from that of a popular entertainer in a broad sense, through to committed communist working in factories, performing to working class audiences. Latterly, after his break with the established Italian communist party, his work has been ideologically related to the 'new left' movement that emerged after the demonstrations of the late 1960s. However, it was during the political movements of the late 1960s that his work was most closely tied with the Italian Communist Party; his break, both ideologically and in practice, came in the 1970s.

His work has never rested easily in the prevalent categories of post war European theatre, particularly the dominant manifestations of 1970s British left wing theatre represented by such writers as Howard Brenton, Edward Bond and David Edgar. Perhaps the only British theatre maker that in any way comes close to the popular tradition of Dario Fo is John McGrath, particularly his work with the *7:84* company[15].

The early phase of his work was in collaboration with the Italian actress Franca Rame (to whom he was once married), and drew largely on material and techniques from nineteenth-century farce, as well as from modes of popular entertainment. Although satirical in

14. Dario Fo has, however, demonstrated *commedia dell'arte* techniques and mask work in some of his one-man performances.

15. *7:84*. The title is taken from the statistic that claims that 7% of the British population owns 84% of the wealth.

its nature, this period of work was not in any real sense, overtly political or leftist. During the political demonstrations of the 1960s, Fo and Franca Rame formed the company *Nuova Scena* in association with the Communist Party. The general sense of the work drew on Bertolt Brecht's concept of the *Lehrstück*. The *Lehrstück* is often translated as 'teaching play'. However a translation closer in spirit to the purpose of the *Lehrstück* is the idea of 'learning play'. The subtle difference between 'teaching' and 'learning' through theatre is important. For both Brecht and Fo, the theatrical methodology was intended to expose problems and by so doing, enable the audience to make certain decisions. This was as opposed to a more didactic agit-prop technique of 'telling' the audience what to think.

In this period, Fo produced works with titles such as *The Worker Knows 300 Words, The Boss 1,000; That's Why He's The Boss* and *Can't Pay? Won't Pay!* The latter play portrays a group of Milanese women who 'liberate' goods from a supermarket as a protest against inflationary measures. However, this period of his work is probably best known for his one-man show, *Mistero Buffo. Buffo* is not in fact a play in the conventional sense, but a series of sketches based upon acts traditionally performed by medieval minstrels. Fo here is deliberately foregrounding the role of the performer in aligning himself with a popular tradition led by performers, rather than often is the case in much of Europe, the playwright (and more recently the director) as *auteur*. This emphasis on the popular performer in much of his work (as opposed to the actor of plays in formal theatres) is as intrinsic to his radical ideology as is the politics derived from Marx, or more locally and precisely Antonio Gramsci[16].

The presentational form of the *Mistero Buffo* pieces drew heavily on an audience/performer relationship more familiar to the stand-up comedian, than to the actor, who certainly since the nineteenth century, has become increasingly isolated from his/her audience. This isolation is both physical and cultural with the members of the audience isolated in the darkened auditorium, while the seamless narrative unfolds before them. How like reading a novel going to the theatre has become since the 1880s. Fo, like Brecht and many twentieth-century cabaret performers of this century, seeks to break through the 'terrifying gulf of the orchestra pit'[17]. An amusing, but telling anecdote relating to one of Fo's *Buffo* performances gives a good account of the open cultural dynamics between performer and audience, that was sought after by Fo.

16. Antonio Gramsci (imprisoned by Mussolini's fascists) is an important figure in the development of socialist thought in the latter half of this century. Most widely disseminated are the editions of his prison notebooks.

17. I believe that Constantin Stanislavski, among others, made a similar statement.

There was one telling moment in the course of the dialogue between the drunk and the angel, which is part of Mistero Buffo, when a woman got to her feet to start shouting. She was getting annoyed with the angel who would not let the drunk get on with his story, and yelled: 'Let him talk, you bastard! Otherwise, I'll come up there and give you a kick in the halo.' The amazing thing was that she was raging at the character whom I had sketched out in the air; she was pointing at the spot where I had left him. Another patient got up and shouted out: 'Nurse, will you stop it?'

The angel had been transformed into the day to day authority they had to deal with[18].

The performance had taken place in a Turin psychiatric hospital. The point is that the nature of Fo's performance and its relationship with the audience encourages (and indeed enables) the audience to enter into an active relationship with the moment of theatre. The audience becomes an expert, because of how the individuals relate the action to their own realities, and become collaborators in an open-ended practice, rather than the passive consumers of a finished art object[19].

Franca Rame

Franca Rame would be ill-served (to say the least) if she was mentioned only in terms of her husband's work. She came from a family of popular entertainers, whose sole ambition was located in the popular 'entertainment business'. Rame however, offers a clear-sighted, theoretical articulation of her work within popular theatre. It was Rame rather than Fo, who saw the full theoretical possibilities in her husband's work, as much as she did in her own.

One criticism levelled against Fo is that although his work does challenge the forms and relationships of bourgeois theatre, by not being fully theorised, it often offers only the delight in the art of the conjuror and does not reach out beyond the stage. Fo quotes an incident in Argentina after a performance of his piece *Trumpets and Raspberries* (1981):

> She (a member of the audience after the performance) started by accusing the whole La Commune company of organising events that are often coldly mechanistic, and have little to do with theatre, and do not reach out beyond the stage .... The barbs were rarely aimed at political targets but at incidents and accidents, and my aim was to distract the audience with the same techniques as some conjuror who prepares away from the audience, the wonderful tricks which will have them all gasping with amazement[20].

Franca Rame in *Tricks of the Trade* theorises the theatre in which she and Fo are involved in general terms, relating much of what she has to say to Bertolt Brecht's concept of the epic[21]. However, beyond this a more particular argument relates Rame's theorising of feminism and comedy to the theatre. In a volume such as this, the interest is in the role that theatre has played in the development of post-war European consciousness; it is therefore interesting to note Rame's relating of her feminism to sexual (as opposed to gender) identity and the potentiality of comedy. What Rame has to say on this subject reveals the process by which ideological similarities across Europe, may undergo significant changes, in a move from northern European cultures to Mediterranean cultures and vice versa.

Her examples are drawn from Mediterranean cultures and focus on the role of women in the theatre. In ancient pre-Hellenic theatre, she argues, women were banned from any level of involvement in

18. Fo, D. *The Tricks of the Trade*. trans. Farrell, J. London: Methuen. 1991, p.190.
19. This point has been argued by many: Bertolt Brecht, Walter Benjamin, Terry Eagleton, Antonio Gramsci, Raymond Williams are notable in this field.
20. Franca Rame, in Fo, D. *The Tricks of the Trade*. trans. Farrell, J. London: Methuen. 1991, p.196.
21. *Ibid.* p.199.

theatre. However, there is a tradition in ancient Mediterranean cultures through to modern times, of the women minstrels and Italian traditions of the bawd in storytelling. She is quite precise in the way that she presents the argument, dispensing immediately with what she regards as the new prudery and denial of sexuality that she perceives in the 'radical' feminisms of northern Europe, as well as the objectification of women's bodies for no reason other than to titillate an audience.

Inevitably, the role of the women minstrels arose because it was the only role allowed them by male dominated cultures. Rame's argument turns on the methods by which the women of different ages exploited the space allowed to them, in order to subvert the enclosing ideology. This perception of course bears a direct relevance to our contemporary world, just as it has done so throughout history. Today, perhaps more so than at any other time, the task of the radical is to locate the moment of potential subversion, rather than to seek revolution on a grand scale. Specifically, Rame sees the role of the woman as bawd in just this light. It is a role where women deliberately use their sexuality to provoke, rather than titillate; to reach out to an audience in conspiracy, rather than to be enclosed as sex objects. The women storytellers in Baccaccio's *Decameron*, she reminds us, are the ones generally in control and 'their stories are more erotically entertaining and spicy than those of their male counterparts'[22].

Her argument is a critique of 'naturalism'. This, at first glance, seems to be a fairly conventional comment on the convention of theatre, that by its reliance on illusion, can only represent an enclosed social totality, maintaining that this view of reality is indeed reality itself. The problem perceived by Rame, is for theatre to be able to reach out to its audience. She argues that the best tool for this task is as it has always been, self-reflexive comedy. The idea of self-reflexivity is important here; to simply make people laugh is not enough. For the audience to merely enjoy themselves, indeed to laugh at the expense of the sense of the play, is to miss the point. Pantomime, in its various manifestations, should not undermine either the play, or the dignity of the performer. Rame argues that in many senses the history of clowning and the mime, such as the white-faced *pierrot*, has been a history of castrating women. For Rame, it should be a question of self-conscious style and comment.

> It is not a matter of prudery. I am in complete agreement with those who are struggling for liberation, once and for all, from those senseless inhibitions on sexual matters which have been inculcated into over the years, but I would always, even when dropping my knickers, like to achieve that with a minimum of style[23].

Conclusions

In an attempt to consolidate the arguments pursued in this, the first part of *Theatre and Europe*, it may be of use to mention briefly the

22. *Ibid.* p.200.
23. *Ibid.* p.201.

work of experimental theatre in the Netherlands in the 1960s and 1970s. By so doing, some of the issues that will be raised as we progress towards the later decades of Europe, will be contextualised. Certainly, the more recent decades of Europe have seen movements away from readily recognised conventions in the theatre, towards 'mixed-media' events, involving the visual arts, dance and music. Emanating from what is often referred to as the 'fringe', collective experiments in performance art have moved more and more towards the centre of cultural concern in Western European culture. This move to the notional centre of culture is, in reality, more a question of appropriation of radical emergent forces by the hegemonic structures of western societies. There are many examples, not least those being the production of Shakespeare in the British theatre of the 1970s. However, we may locate the two important elements that challenged theatrical conventions in the 1960s as being in the Netherlands.

The challenge was ideological and was centred in two central practices: the use of space and the nature of theatrical production, with particular reference to the role of the director. The *Mickery-theater* was established in 1965 by Ritsaert Ten Cate in his farmhouse in Loenersloot, a village near to Amsterdam. In 1970 the *Mickery-theater* moved to a converted cinema in Amsterdam. The salient feature of the theatre building is that there are no fixed areas dedicated to audience or performers. A familiar convention now established in a small number of theatre buildings in the 1990s, was then a radical break with architectural developments of perspective scenography, that had been evolving since the late sixteenth century in England and even earlier in Italy. The nature of the performing space in both the physical and social sense, was devised in an appropriate manner to the demands of the performance. While hosting many experimental groups in the late 1960s and 70s, such as *La Mama* from New York, *The Pip Simmons Theatre Group* of London and *Tenjo Tsukiji* of Tokyo, the *Mickery-theater* produced its own pieces, increasingly exploring the nature of the relationship between fiction (theatre) and reality.

Appropriately, the other movement in the Netherlands at approximately the same time, was the *Aktie Tomaat*. This movement is translated as 'Action Tomato' or the 'Tomato Campaign', after the events of late 1969, when tomatoes were thrown at actors during a performance by the *Nederlandse Comedie* at the municipal theatre of Amsterdam. *Aktie Tomaat* was appropriate in the sense that while the *Mickery-theater* was challenging hegemonic conventions regarding theatrical space, the *Aktie Tomaat* protest challenged the authoritarian status of the director. The main thrust of development in post–war European theatre has been centred in the rise of the director as *auteur*. The notable theatrical developments of the 1970s and 1980s saw the actors attempting to regain a voice in the creative act of theatre. The role of the director has not been substantially changed in many large subsidised theatres throughout Western Europe, but in the smaller companies, those arguably in the vanguard of theatrical experiment, a distinctly collective ideology of theatre making has emerged.

The protest of the *Aktie Tomaat* was led by students of the Amsterdam School of Drama *(Toneelschool)* and was a part of that broader movement throughout the United States of America (anti-Vietnam-war campus demonstrations) and Western Europe in the late 1960s. The call in the theatre, as it was on the broader political front, was for more democracy. Specifically, in the theatre, the demonstrations voiced discontent with the kind of director who, who seeing 'himself' as *auteur*, drew heavily on the inspiration of Edward Gordon Craig in the treatment of actors as *übermarionettes*, subject to the will of the individual interpretative vision.

In one sense these 'biographies' of individuals and theatre companies seem to be dealt with in isolation, with little in-depth analysis of the detail of their particular circumstances. However, while sacrificing that element, the intention has been to pick out instances in post-war cultural history as moments of significance, or signposts, the purpose of which was to signal points by which a debate may be enjoined.

The call may read as one for theatre to become more socially relevant and in the next section, which historically allows us to consider developments in British theatre (once the UK had joined the then styled Common Market), we will be able to examine the wide spread of theatre groups which espoused a collective methodology of work, with an overt political agenda.

The Entry of The United Kingdom to the Single Europe Act: 1973–1986

The entry of the United Kingdom into the European Community in 1973 was, as we still know in the mid-1990s, fraught with difficulties and complexity. The United Kingdom's relationship with rest of Europe has never been easy, but theatre seems to focus very clearly on this perceived disparity of culture. While the United Kingdom's entry allows us, in this volume, to consider the growth of British theatre post 1973, it also allows the possibility of seeing that the most interesting developments in theatre in this country are inextricably tied to the influences of all that had been developed in the rest of Europe, during the first half of the twentieth century.

The culture that is claimed to be exclusively British (or even English) and serves as the bedrock for right-wing anti-Europeanism, has also relied heavily — and ironically in the vitality of British theatre — upon the experiments and innovations of European cultural practices for its very dynamism. This chapter will look at the development of British theatre in the 1970s and 1980s, both in terms of the development of the large national subsidised theatre companies and the left-wing fringe companies. The specific focus will be on the ideological inter-relationship between the established theatres and the radical fringe. In particular, an attempt will be made to delineate the processes by which the innovations of European and other cultures were simultaneously an influence on, and subject to, ideological appropriation by the various branches of post-war British theatre.

Shakespeare, Brecht and the *Other Place*

Although the *Royal Shakespeare Company* has played a significant role in post-war European theatre, it is not the intention of this book to focus too closely on that Company's work. The purpose of a broad analysis of the development of European consciousness will be well served by focusing on two salient features of the *RSC*: the influence of certain European practitioners on the contemporary dissemination of Shakespeare on the English stage; and the innovatory work of Buzz Goodbody, the first woman director to be employed by the *RSC* and the founder of their experimental performance space in the 1970s.

It is possible to argue that, in a curious way, the ideas of theatre production as articulated by the German playwright and director, Bertolt Brecht, offer the contemporary practitioner of Elizabethan drama an insight into the nature of the theatrical event of the late sixteenth century. Brecht, in his materialist analysis of theatre, sought through the concept of *Verfremdung*, to subvert illusion in order that (a) the fictional character may be located historically/socially and that (b) the audience, freed from a situation where empathy with an illusion of passion was the only means of relating to the events on the stage, would be in a position to observe the contradictions of life. He enabled the audience to observe the potential alternative realities of a given historical moment, rather than being persuaded through fictional illusion that this is how life is (a social totality).

In *The Messingkauf Dialogues*, Brecht draws on a sense of the Elizabethan theatre performance as such an open-ended cultural event[1]. From the late 1960s and well into the 1970s, the stages of the *RSC* opened up, projecting themselves through the picture frame of the proscenium arch in an attempt to create a more direct, illusion-breaking, contact with the audience. The old traditions of pictorial scenography and acting styles gave way to a form that attempted to speak directly to its audience as a part of a mode of politicising the reading of the play. This style of presentation, while recalling some elements of what we assume the experience of the public playhouse in the sixteenth century to have been like, owed a lot to the dramaturgy and theatrical practices of Bertolt Brecht. However, while Brecht may have been a significant influence in terms of a more open style of performance, the English practice became more a question of a liberal appropriation of Brecht's outward imagery, while denying the political ideology that informed such practice.

There were many different ideologies informing the practices of the *RSC* in the 1970s, often giving rise to conflicting identities of the Institution. Since its inception in 1959, the *RSC* has been criticised by both left and right wing politicians and, like many efficient liberal institutions, it has survived and renewed itself by absorbing, rather than repressing, that which challenged its mainstream work. Significant in this area was the work of Buzz Goodbody in the early 1970s. Goodbody joined the *RSC* straight from work primarily with student theatre and Fringe street theatre. Her appointment came about from a meeting with John Barton (one of the directors of the *RSC* and ex Cambridge English academic) at the *Twelfth Annual National Students/Sunday Times Drama Festival*. He offered her a job as his personal assistant, which in the (still) male dominated *RSC*, turned out to be more a matter of being his personal nursemaid.

> Barton was not looking for a 'nine-to-five typist', as he puts it. He was only interested in 'a 'Girl Friday' slave and companion, but university-trained, who was keen on theatre, and Buzz was the first such 'dogsbody' whom Barton took on[2].

She progressed to the point where she was asked to act as assistant director for the whole Stratford season in 1969. By and large this was an inappropriate move for Goodbody and her work was met with less than sympathetic reviews. We may argue with some justification

1. Brecht, B. *The Messingkauf Dialogues* trans. Willett, J. London: Methuen. 1965.
2. Chambers, C. *Other Spaces.* London: Methuen. 1980, p.26.

that the radical approaches to the received texts of Shakespeare, incorporating popular imagery into the theatrical realisation, did not rest easily in the English vision of how the national poet should be represented. Though possibly at a less sophisticated level, Goodbody was setting out a similar cultural polemic that the more 'European' directors such as Brook, Strehler and Stein were to accomplish.

The *RSC* was, in the early 1970s, considering the possibility of opening a second Stratford auditorium. The outcome of this planning strategy was a theatre space now known as the *Other Place* and which became the physical and cultural site of Goodbody's true worth as a director[3]. The *Other Place* had originally been a rehearsal space a couple of hundred metres up the road from the *Shakespeare Memorial Theatre* and had occasionally been used for informal performances. From this unlikely beginning arose, under the initial leadership of Buzz Goodbody, one of the most interesting experimental theatre spaces in Europe in the early 1970s.

Colin Chambers argues that Goodbody found herself unable to articulate her theatre in the way that the demands of the 'big stage' required, with actors using 'big stage' techniques. 'She was resorting to spectacle, to rhetoric, to pastiche, and that was not the answer'[4]. Likewise, Terry Hands, then one of the Directors of the *RSC*, said:

> ...It was simply an idea of making theatre more immediate in a circumstance which was, in terms of stage craft, much easier to control. Working on a big proscenium arch stage involves areas of craft and technique that are totally unnecessary when working in a space like the *Other Place*. It was simply a way of allowing the audience to be right on top of a performance ... [5]

However, Goodbody offered a 'manifesto' for the *Other Place* that included such considerations as 'reaching a new audience as Theatregoround had tried to do and serving the community'[6]. Goodbody's intention was ideological as well as practical. She wished to broaden the audience for the *RSC*, 'for artistic as well as social reasons'[7].

Without doubt the most celebrated production that emerged from the early experiments was Buzz Goodbody's direction of *Hamlet* with Ben Kingsley in the title role. Peter Thomson's review of this production in 1975 doubts if the production should be referred to as Buzz Goodbody's; not from any doubt as to her contribution, but more to highlight the egalitarian nature of her relationship with actors during the rehearsal process[8]. The rise of the director in post-war Europe has seen the power of the director, as *auteur*, in theatre increase, as is clearly exemplified in the work of Peter Stein and Giorgio Strehler. Goodbody's methods, in part coming out of her radical leftist political ideology, but also from her initial experiences on the big stage of the main theatre, led her towards a more collaborative methodology of making theatre.

Hamlet was set in modern dress in the tiny and austere acting space provided by the *Other Place*. Most people who saw the

3. 'th' other place', *Hamlet* Act 4, Sc 3, line 33.
4. *op. cit.* Chambers. p.33.
5. Terry Hands in interview with Christopher McCullough in *The Shakespeare Myth*. Ed. Graham Holderness Manchester: Manchester University Press. 1988, p.125.
6. Theatregoround was the small scale touring section of the *Royal Shakespeare Company*, the intention of which was to take theatre to communities that otherwise would not have such access.
7. *op. cit.* Chambers. p.34.
8. Wells, S. ed. *Shakespeare Survey*. Cambridge: Cambridge University Press. 1975, pp.151-153.

production were excited by its immediacy and direct manner of communication. What excited the reviewer Peter Thomson (and many others) was the honest speaking of the lines and 'the constant testing of the sound of the words against their meaning'[9]. His view was that Goodbody had coaxed the play into the hands of the actors. The two significant points that may be drawn from this event are: the potential of reclaiming of the text by the actors and the potential of the intimate theatre space to make a virtue of its lack of elaborate scenography. The idea of actors reclaiming a text goes back to theories concerning the manner by which the plays of Elizabethan dramatists reached the point of performance. As we are aware, the concept of the director comes to us from the nineteenth century. Before that period, and in particular the instance of the popular Elizabethan theatre, it is thought that the actors worked as an ensemble without the exterior guiding handing of the director. Many theatre scholars see in this a virtue whereby a 'truer' meaning of the play may be achieved. What is certain is that Goodbody's method of work foregrounded the presence of the actors over the other elements that have become so pre-eminent in the theatre. Sadly, shortly after the production opened, Buzz Goodbody committed suicide.

Peter Brook and Interculturalism

The move of Peter Brook, the British theatre director known for his 'radical' readings of Shakespeare, from London to Paris in 1970, provides an interesting and complex feature in the idea of cultural exchange between those cultures that were, increasingly, finding themselves heading towards the ideal of a federal European state, in their post-colonial phase.

Peter Brook first attracted attention as an undergraduate at the University of Oxford with, what were then regarded as, adventurous productions of Shakespeare's plays; both at the University and in small London theatre clubs. He was almost immediately taken up, in the 1940s, by the ailing *Shakespeare Memorial Theatre Summer Season*. Very quickly he gained the reputation as an *enfant terrible*, largely on the basis of his willingness to take on the role of polemical director. Of most significance for this context, was Brook's assimilation of 'other' European influences that ranged, often seemingly in a contradictory fashion, from Antonin Artaud (France) to Bertolt Brecht (Germany).

Perhaps however, the most significant influence on Brook's work in his English years, particularly in the 1960s, was that of the Polish critic Jan Kott. What Kott offered as a thesis, and was taken up by Peter Brook and others such as Peter Hall, was the notion that Shakespeare was our 'contemporary'[10]. Briefly, the argument pursues the idea that Shakespeare's universal genius was/is such that it transcends the materiality of history. Implicit in this argument is the denial of a materialist analysis that locates consciousness in its historical context, arguing instead that, in the case of Shakespeare,

9. Peter Thomson's review in *Shakespeare Survey*. Cambridge: Cambridge University Press. 1975, p.153.

10. Jan Kott prosecuted this argument in his book, *Shakespeare our Contemporary*. London: Methuen. 1965.

the values of the plays are for all times[11]. In a sense Kott's thesis may be seen as a reversal of the argument articulated by Marx in the Preface of *A Contribution to the Critique of Political Economy*, where he argues that ... life determines consciousness determining life. Shakespeare then can be for example, in Kott's terms, an existentialist in *King Lear*[12]. This approach has been taken up by many other British directors. Perhaps most notable is Michael Bogdanov, in, amongst others, his production of *The Taming of the Shrew*, where he argues the case for Shakespeare being a feminist[13]. This is not necessarily a denial of the existence of gender politics in sixteenth-century England; more an argument that seeks to afford Shakespeare a consciousness transcendent of his historical context.

Brook moved to Paris in 1970, at a time, many critics would say, when his most famous Shakespeare production, *A Midsummer Night's Dream* was being applauded around the world. The reactions to Brook's production of this play relate closely to the reasons for his loosening of ties with the *RSC* and his subsequent move to Paris. Brook saw this production as part of a long process of work that included his experiments in the 1960s with Artaud's ideas of *The Theatre of Cruelty* and the influence of the Polish director Jerzy Grotowski.

While Artaud had not produced any theatre of great significance, Grotowski had established his theatre laboratory in Poland. Grotowski's purpose was to research, through a 'psycho-physical' technique, what he perceived as the 'spiritual' essence of theatre, freed from the constraints of technology and the whole commercial apparatus that had, increasingly, formed the determining factor in the nature of performance since the emergence of the public playhouses in sixteenth-century England. Brook felt that the constraint of working in a large subsidised theatre, such as the *RSC*, with limited time for rehearsal schedules, was too restrictive and reliant on contemporary theatre technology. His move to Paris was initiated by an invitation, in 1968, from Jean-Louis Barrault for Brook to work as a part of the *Théâtre des Nations*. This experience offered Brook the opportunity to work with actors from many different cultures and resulted in him establishing what was initially known as a *Centre of Theatre Research*, but latterly had added the nomenclature, *Centre of Creation*.

> From the start, the word 'centre' seemed to correspond with what we needed. At first, we set up a Centre of Research, then later we added a Centre of Creation, which were two names for an overlapping series of activities. We felt that research in the theatre needs constantly to be put to the test in performance and performing, and needs all the time and conditions it demands — and which a professional company can seldom afford[14].

The establishing of the *International Centre of Theatre Research*, as it eventually came to be named, is significant, not only in terms of the development of attitudes towards the practice of theatre in post-war

11. The tradition of according Shakespeare a semi-mythical status may be traced back to the English Romantics and later in the nineteenth century (even back to Garrick).

12. *op. cit.* Kott, J. 'King Lear or Endgame' in *Shakespeare our Contemporary*. p.100.

13. See Michael Bogdanov interviewed by Christopher McCullough in *The Shakespeare Myth*. Holderness, G. ed. Manchester: Manchester University Press. 1988, pp.87-95.

14. Brook, P. 'The International Centre' in *The Shifting Point*. London: Methuen. 1988, p.105.

Europe, but also in the wider context of Europe's cultural relationships with the rest of the post-colonial world. Brook is at great pains to articulate his desire for theatre research to reach across nations and cultures; for there to be an exchange of cultures that reaches not for what he refers to as the 'the culture itself', but 'what is behind it'[15].

Brook's intentions were straightforward in that he wished for an exchange between cultures; for his theatre not to bound by a form of Euro-centrism, any more than it was to be in servitude to a top-heavy theatre technology. However, his mode of language, and certain aspects of his practice, reveal a more complex problem. Many of the countries with whom the European nations deal, on an economic and political level, are also those countries that were, until relatively recently, those whose inhabitants were colonised by Europe. His rejection of the complex technological structures of theatre institutions led to a curious choice of performance site that often involved (as will be described later in this section) a distressed décor. The problem for those theatre practitioners, like Peter Brook, is related to the nature of the political/cultural relationship that is possible between and within cultures.

One of the most significant influences on the work of Brook, since the establishment of the *International Centre of Theatre Research*, has been that of Asian cultures, in particular the Indian sub-continent. Indeed, if we examine the influences of a number of the European *avant garde*, such as Eugenio Barba (Sweden/Italy), Antonin Artaud and Jerzy Grotowski, the source of much of their practice has been drawn from Asian countries. The question that is pertinent in this context must relate to problems emanating from a nineteenth- century European view of Asia and Africa — a view that simultaneously exploited and celebrated those cultures as mysterious and exotic, or dark and forbidding[16]. Curiously, Japan, while equally being seen as a source for what is 'exotic' in theatre culture, is designated as a country, and not given the generic title of a continent. While Africa and Africans are just that, irrespective of their country or culture, the continental designation serving for all the cultures and countries.

> Our first task was to try and put an end to the stereotypes, but certainly not to reduce everyone to a neutral anonymity. Stripped of his ethnic mannerisms a Japanese becomes more Japanese, an African more African, and a point is reached where new forms of behaviour and expression are no longer predictable. A new situation emerges which enables of all origins to create together, and what they create takes on a colour of its own. This is not unlike what happens in a piece of orchestral music, where each sound keeps its identity while merging into a new event[17].

Whether it is Japan's economic power in the world that allows its status to be defined as a country, over the countries of Africa and India to be subsumed into the identity of continent, we cannot be sure. However, this small point does act as key into the relationship

15. *Ibid.* p.106.
16. We have only to recall the writings of Sir Richard Burton or Joseph Conrad's short novel, *The Heart of Darkness.*
17. *op. cit.* Brook. p.106.

that Peter Brook (and other European directors who equally seek the oriental otherness in non-western theatre) establishes with other cultures. We cannot avoid the conclusion that the perceived mystique of eastern cultures defines them as being 'other', while Europe, as the known quantity, carries implication that it is the norm[18].

By far the most interesting recent analysis of the cultural relationships between European countries and those they once colonised has been made by Rustom Bharucha, working and living in India as a writer, director and dramaturg[19]. Bharucha is of particular interest when we attempt to analyse the development of post-war European theatre and culture, precisely because he is not a European. As an Indian whose command of English is informed by the legacy of the British Raj, he occupies a complex position from which he is able to interrogate the fascination that many European directors have had with what has been termed the Orient. We may trace this construction of the Orient as something exotic back to such figures as Sir Richard Burton and, perhaps nearer to this subject, the figures of E. Gordon Craig and Antonin Artaud. Drawing on Susan Sontag's essay on Antonin Artaud, Bharucha focuses on what appears to be Artaud's fascination with a perceived mystical world (the Orient), that offers a pathway for spiritual/aesthetic renewal, that has been driven out of European thought and experience over the last four hundred years[20]. In his essay *No More Masterpieces* Artaud calls for a rejection of the cerebral and the psychological obsessions of modern theatre.

> Because for four hundred years, that is since the Renaissance, we have become accustomed to purely descriptive, narrative theatre, narrating psychology[21].

Sontag and Bharucha both argue that, for Artaud, the stimulus of Balinese theatre (his experience of which was limited to seeing a Balinese group dance at a Paris exhibition) could well have been, 'the theatre of a Dahomey tribe or the Shamanistic ceremonies of the Patagonian Indians. What counts is that the other culture be genuinely other; that is, non-western, non-contemporary'[22]. The sense is that Artaud's search is not so much for a full understanding of other cultures, but for inspiration for his non-cerebral, ahistorical, 'theatre of Dreams'. 'The "oriental theatre" was a construct for Artaud, not a practice'[23].

Returning to contemporary European theatre we may identify Peter Brook's production of the holy Hindu scripture and history, *Mahabharata*, as a prime example of post-colonial cultural appropriation. Bharucha draws attention to a model by which the 'borrowing' of such works may be seen to be the continuance of the colonial appropriation of raw materials into a post-colonial appropriation of culture. He argues the case that the English originally took raw materials from India, transported them to England where they were made into commodities, and then sold back to people in India. Brook, it is argued, 'does not merely take our

18. The account of his journey, with actors from the *International Centre*, from the northern Mediterranean coast of Algeria, through the Sahara desert and south into Nigeria, is by any terms, a fascinating example of post-colonial assumptions.

19. Bharucha, R. *Theatre and the World: Performance and the Politics of Culture* London: Routledge. 1993.

20. Artaud, A. *Antonin Artaud: Selected Writings.* trans. Weaver, H. with an introductory essay by Sontag, S. New York: Farrar, Strauss & Giroux. 1976.

21. Artaud, A. *The Theatre and its Double.* trans. Corti, V. London: John Calder. 1970, p.75.

22. Bharucha, R. quoting Sontag, S. in *The Theatre and the World.* London: Routledge. 1993, p.14.

23. *Ibid.* p.17.

commodities and textiles and transform them into costumes and props. He has taken one of our most significant texts and decontextualized it from its history in order to sell it to audiences in the West'[24].

Bharucha asks the question, 'What is the *Mahabharata* without Hindu philosophy?'. In one sense this question asks a great deal more than may be supposed at first reading. Apart from the problems being raised on the level of interculturalism, there is the question that crops up again and again regarding the nature of our contemporary readings of ancient texts. It is fairly self-evident that we cannot, for example, share an identical consciousness with the inhabitants of late sixteenth-century England; even if we accept Jan Kott's argument that Shakespeare can transcend history to share the consciousness of all people, at all times. But does the question raised about the Hindu basis of the *Mahabharata* mean that no text may be removed from the ideological base out of which it was formed? There is no simple answer to this question. However, the question that has to be raised in relation to the fascination with the Orient for some European directors, must relate to our understanding of the cultural currency that exists between the appropriating culture and the one from who the borrowing takes place. It may be a fairly straightforward and equal exchange between different European cultures, or for that matter between Britain and the USA. An exchange between two cultures, where the one has been the colonial master for two hundred years, has to be considered in a different perspective.

Peter Brook's work in Paris in many ways is symptomatic of many post-war European ideological obsessions; in particular his choice and treatment of physical performance spaces provide a curious paradigm of the post-modern condition, not unrelated to his mission to replenish the life of western theatre with the life blood of 'oriental mysticism'. For the New York performance of the *Mahabharata,* Brook chose a dilapidated eighty four year old variety theatre. The theatre was renovated at great expense for the performance, not to bring it up to date, but to preserve its sense of decay. Likewise, the *Théâtre aux Bouffes du Nord*, which has been the Paris home of Brook's company since 1974, has been 'renovated' so as to retain the sense of its state of decay and age. As Bharucha points out, 'Only the West could afford to renovate a theatre and then spend more money to make it look old again'[25].

A central tenet of post-modernism is that there is nothing new, only the endless reworking of ideas where art is constantly self-reflexive; where irony and wit emerge from the arch self-consciousness of a theatrical space, drawing attention to its own artifice. The deliberate distressing of the theatrical space is little different from the distressed décor of the imitation French cafe in the local high street, that has carefully nicotine stained walls in order to evoke the atmosphere of the left bank gathering places of French intellectuals. A cynical perspective might state that the now bankrupt western bourgeois culture can only repeatedly deconstruct itself in

24. *Ibid.* p.68.
25. *Ibid.* p.82.

order to renew itself self-reflexively; either that, or 'borrow' from other cultures.

Development of Alternative theatre in Britain

This section, rather than concentrating on the work of individual directors, will attempt to broaden the argument in order to survey the aspects of theatre that dominated activity in the UK during the 1970s. The precedent set by Buzz Goodbody (among many other innovators) in observing the potential of small scale theatre work was developed in a remarkable way by the writers and companies that, emerging from the radicalism of the late 1960s, reached a height of productive activity in the 1970s and early 1980s[26]. The radical movements in the late 1960s, with the Paris demonstrations and the reassessment of Marxist ideology in the light of the Stalinist atrocities in earlier decades, had a profound effect on the thinking of the playwrights and directors, especially those who passed through the new British universities founded by the Wilson Labour government. Of the many individuals and companies that should be mentioned, space in this volume will only allow reference to Howard Brenton and *The Portable Theatre*, David Edgar, Caryl Churchill and *The Joint Stock Theatre Company* and John McGrath and *7:84*. This small selection omits many other important contributions to British/European thatre in the1970s; most notably writers such as Edward Bond. The intention here is only to offer signs on the broad map of European cultural development; in this instance, those individuals whose genesis was in the 'alternative' theatre of the 1970s and 1980s.

Quite what we may define as alternative theatre is a complex issue and may not be limited those individuals who were 'alternative' in that they espoused a leftist ideology. The *Other Place* is a useful example of how the original intention formed under the guidance of Buzz Goodbody was subverted by those who followed her work in that theatre. Certainly Trevor Nunn's production of *Macbeth* was a remarkable reading of the play for the intimate space, but it hardly espoused the same causes as Goodbody's *Hamlet*. Nunn's focus is perhaps best located in the view of the British director, man of letters and medicine, Jonathan Miller. He was enthusiastic about the potential of the small space performance as a cultural site for what he described as the 'chamber classic' — in fact a reversal of the egalitarian ideals espoused by Goodbody. This is what became of the *Other Place*; one may argue that it has been a classic case of liberal appropriation by the main auditorium at Stratford upon Avon. Generally, however, what we identify as alternative theatre in Britain in the 1970s and 1980s, did develop out of the ideals of young men and women caught in the leftist radical cultural maelstrom of the late 1960s. Their development and shifting of ideological position since those years (not always rightwards ideologically) has been debated often and will be referred to later in this chapter.

26. We may trace the genealogy of 'small space' performance experiments back to André Antoine with the *Théâtre Libre* in Paris, in the 1880s.

Howard Brenton

Howard Brenton emerged from the 1960s with all the necessary
credentials afforded to one of those writers in the vanguard of radical
alternative theatre. He came from what would have been identified
then as a working class background, went to grammar school and
then to Cambridge. His early work as a writer may be best
exemplified by the claim that he wished to propel petrol bombs
through the proscenium arch. Quite where the claim originated is
unclear, but certainly we may observe two factors; one of his plays
did include a scene where a character shows the audience, as much
as the other characters, how to make a petrol bomb[27]; and that his
early, and contentiously most agit-prop work, took place anywhere
but in proscenium arch theatres. However, Brenton's work, as it
became more widely known, moved from the small scale spaces to
the large stages and auditoria of the large subsidised theatres, most
notably the *National Theatre of Great Britain*. Put simply, Brenton's
argument is that in the small scale spaces of the alternative theatre
movement, the playwright is, by and large, preaching to the
converted. The move to the large scale theatres means that the
potential for reaching a far wider audience, many of whom represent
a far wider social cross section, is greatly enhanced. We may be
certain that arguments for and against this move represent a well
trodden path[28]. The change in theatrical space for Brenton has not,
in any substantial sense, represented a leaving behind of his earlier
values; indeed in some senses he has become more controversial in
his confrontations.

For the purpose of this volume, a brief history of Brenton's play
The Romans in Britain, will serve well the purpose of gaining a sense
of the broader cultural movement and attitudes that were a part of
the forming of post-war Europe. What makes *The Romans in Britain*
interesting, apart from being a good play and still very much of our
times (it was written in 1980), is the activity that went on around the
first production at *The National Theatre*, and out of that activity the
means by which the play gained its reputation as a play likely to
corrupt the audience. *The Romans in Britain*, in broad terms is
concerned with colonialism and imperialism — the successions of
invasions that created the English and the current occupation of
Ireland. Part I deals with the imminent Roman invasion of these
islands in 54 BC and Part II sets the scene just prior to the Saxon
invasions that resulted in the creation of the English[29]. The first part
concludes by thrusting us into contemporary Northern Ireland and
the end of the play leaves us with a cook deconstructing the
mythology of a golden age that never was. Ironically this
deconstruction is also the moment in which the myth of King
Arthur is made. A myth that in the nineteenth century served well
the construction of modern English cultural hegemony through, for
example, the work of Tennyson.

> FIRST COOK: Actually he was a king who never was. His
> Government was the people of Britain. His peace was as common

27. This scene occurs in
    Howard Brenton's play
    Fruit which was
    written in 1970 and
    designed to be toured
    at the time of the
    1970 General
    Election.
28. In particular Bull, J.
    *New British Political
    Dramatists*. London:
    Methuen. 1984.
29. *Ibid*. p.204.

as rain or sun. His law was as natural as grass, growing in a meadow. And there never was a Government, or a peace, or a law like that ... And when he was dead, the King who never was and the Government that never was — were mourned. And remembered. Bitterly. And thought of as a golden age, lost and yet to come ... What was his name?

SECOND COOK: ... Er — any old name. Arthur? Arthur?

The play is about colonisation; about the myths created by people in order to hide the harsh realities of their actions. It is also about the myths that may be created around plays.

Given that colonisation is rape of one country by another, so Brenton wished to carry the metaphor to all levels of human relationship. In Part I when three Roman soldiers come across the celtic youths bathing naked they see them as 'wogs', the 'natural' term of colonial abuse. After a short skirmish one of the Roman soldiers attempts an anal rape on one of the celtic youths. The rape fails because the boy has haemorrhoids. The action of attempted rape lasts about thirty seconds and has been the sole cause of the play's notoriety. During a performance of the original production in London, the then Leader of the Greater London Council (since disbanded by the Thatcher Government when it became dominated by the political left) Sir Horace Cutler, walked out disgusted by what he saw. Attempts to close the production were made, under the Theatres Act of 1968, but none succeeded; or at least they didn't in terms of conviction. In designating the play as being about something that it was not, they did succeed.

> This Act applies to all stage performances and it provides by section 8 that no obscenity prosecution may be instituted in England or Wales arising from a performance of a play 'except by or with the consent of the Attorney General'[30].

Eventually Mrs Mary Whitehouse, a well known campaigner against what she sees to be the moral decline of this country, sought to bring a private prosecution against Michael Bogdanov (the Director of the play) under Section 16 of the Theatres Act, on the grounds that the play was obscene. The Director of Public Prosecutions investigated the complaint and reported that no prosecution was likely to succeed. Thereupon, the Attorney General not only refused to launch a prosecution, but also refused to consent to a private prosecution being brought by Mrs Mary Whitehouse. The only grounds upon which this could be achieved would entail proving that the play was obscene.

The Director of the play was subsequently prosecuted by Whitehouse under Section 13 of the 1956 Sexual Offences Act which makes it an offence for a man (*sic*) to procure an act of gross indecency with another man. The trial judge held that there was a *prima facie* case to the particular performance, although the

30. Geoffrey Robertson, junior counsel to Michael Bogdanov, Director of *The Romans in Britain* at the National Theatre, in a letter to Christopher McCullough.

proceedings were effectively nullified when the Attorney filed a *nolle prosequi*. In England and Wales we are left with a number of unresolved questions: namely whether Section 13 has any applicability at all to a simulated stage production and whether discussion between a director and two willing actors amounts to an act of 'procuration'.

On one level we may assume that there was a curious confusion between some individual's notions of the differences between fiction and reality. Whatever way the case is viewed, the damage has been done. The play ceased, in the popular mind to be about colonisation and identity, but became very simply a play about anal rape. About two years later, the English and Drama Department of University College Swansea attempted to produce *The Romans in Britain* in the *Dylan Thomas Theatre*. They were banned by both the City of Swansea and the University College from performing the play in public, despite the solicitor of the *National Theatre* going to Swansea with Michael Bogdanov, Howard Brenton and the Theatre's Anglican chaplain, and giving a press conference. This ban was based on the grounds of the play's notoriety as likely to deprave, and not on the grounds of its political ideology. The cultural making of the play's mythology had been achieved by the right-wing attempted prosecution. Howard Brenton wrote to *The Guardian* newspaper in defence of the University College students' attempt to produce the play. It is worth quoting in part:

> ...An amateur production of my play *The Romans in Britain* has been banned in Swansea. It was to have been performed in the *Dylan Thomas Theatre* ... The loose-bowelled, tin-pot cultural Stalins running the *Dylan Thomas Theatre* should beware. I day-dream that Thomas would have understood *The Romans in Britain*. But I am certain of what his ghost thinks of the people who have banned it under his name: he curses them ... The curse of a great dead Welsh poet is not easy to bear. They can lift it by painting their building yellow and renaming it the Mary Whitehouse Theatre. His ghost would never gaunt such a flea-pit. Or they can simply turn round on the local hysteria and let Swansea University perform the play ... Meanwhile they have my contempt.

Best wishes,
Howard Brenton[31].

While the radical (leftist) element of Brenton's work concentrates more on content perhaps, than on experiments with dramatic form and context of performance, Caryl Churchill and John McGrath both, in different ways, have drawn significantly on the theories and practices of Bertolt Brecht. Brenton, although his plays do seem to possess an epic quality similar to that of Brecht, has said, in the case of *Epsom Downs*, that he is more interested in a kind of super naturalism on a grand scale[32]. In their very different ways Churchill and McGrath are redefining both the structure and context of their work.

31. Brenton, H. *The Guardian*. 1993.
32. From an unpublished interview with Phillip Roberts (University of Sheffield).

Caryl Churchill and the *Joint Stock Theatre Company*

While wishing to avoid fitting people into categories that are too easy and tend towards the simplistic, it would be accurate to see Churchill's work coming from a broadly socialist/feminist perspective[33]. This of course is over simplifying her ideology and her more recent work, such as *The Skriker* (1994) has revealed a new interest in the direction of performance art, particularly in her collaborations with the dancer/choreographer Ian Spink. The theme that is most relevant to this study, with its emphasis on the European context, is best exemplified by Churchill's work with the *Joint Stock Theatre Company* in the 1970s — specifically the collaboration that produced the play *Cloud Nine*. This play, in many ways is similar in preoccupations to *The Romans in Britain*. Here there is the sense that the subject matter focuses on notions of colonisation and the attendant myths. However, *Cloud Nine* is more radical in its treatment of historical narrative through dramatic structure. Brenton's play, although it moves backwards and forwards through history, interweaves the scenes into a tight pattern that almost conflates history. *Cloud Nine* treats the movement through history in a more episodic manner. The scenes of nineteenth-century British colonial African occupation are juxtaposed against the scenes that are set in contemporary Britain. Furthermore, the characters and the actors interchange in such a way as to expose historical contradictions in a dialectical form.

The play had its genesis in collective method of the *Joint Stock Theatre Company*. The company was prominent in the 1970s and early 1980s, but in the late 1980s the economic recession, combined with government antipathy to small, seemingly 'alternative' theatre companies, meant that by the early 1990s their Arts Council subsidy had been removed. This financial disenfranchisement signalled the end of one of the most productive companies in contemporary British theatre. Their work method was that of the collective; a project would start with workshops in which the writer, director and actors researched a particular topic. The writer then took ideas produced through improvisation and worked on them, returning to the company for the rehearsal period. This process went on until the play/production was ready for performance. 'In the case of *Cloud Nine*, the workshop lasted for three weeks, the initial writing period for twelve, and the rehearsal/rewrite for six'[34].

The first Act of *Cloud Nine* takes place in Victorian colonial Africa. The father of the family, Clive, heads a firm unyielding structure, wherein women and children have patriarchal values firmly imposed upon them. The values of the family may be equated with the imperialistic values of colonial Africa. The sexuality of individuals, especially women, children and homosexuals, is vigorously denied; as is, of course African racial identity. Act Two is set a hundred years in the future, with the same characters, but with everyone having aged only twenty five years. The historical analysis of Act One is exchanged for 'a collage of new life-styles in London in the 1970s'[35].

33. Wandor, M. *Carry on the Understudies: Theatre and Sexual Politics.* London: Routledge. 1981.

34. Churchill, C. *Cloud Nine.* London: Pluto Press. 1979, p.3.

35. *op. cit.* Wandor. p.171.

Although the two historical periods are linked by many of the same characters appearing in both parts, Churchill keeps the relationship a dialectical one by the simple device of cross gender and cross age casting. The family of Act One comprises:

> Clive the paterfamilias, Betty his wife played by a man because she wants to be what men want her to be, and in the same way, Joshua, the black servant, is played by a white man because he wants to be what whites want him to be. Betty does not value herself as a woman, nor does Joshua value himself as a black. Edward, Clive's son, is played by a woman for a different reason, partly to do with the stage convention of having boys played by women (Peter Pan, radio plays etc.) and partly to do with highlighting the way Clive tries to impose traditional male behaviour on him[36].

Other characters are marginalised or reviled, as in the homosexuality of Ellen and Harry. The change over to Act Two finds all the characters played by the same gender, with the one exception of Cathy aged five, who is played by the actor who plays Clive in the first half. Churchill's reasoning for this choice is partly to reverse the choice of having Edward, Clive's son played by a girl in Act One, and in part because, she argues, the size and presence of a man on stage seemed appropriate to the emotional force of a young child.

Michelene Wandor argues that Act Two lacks the cause and effect of the 'historical' first half and has, as its emphasis, a liberalised situation in which individuals deal with their own lives in 'a sharp and moving way'. However, she argues, while sexual taboos about lesbianism and libertarian lifestyles are broken (particularly in the group sex scene on stage), there is no particular political analysis of the whys and wherefores of the action.

> The speed and wit of the first half structurally reinforce the socialist-feminist dynamic of the interconnection between class and gender. In the second half the libertarian lifestyles demonstrate the radical feminist dynamic of women determining their own sexuality and ways of living. But the second half lacks any sense of class (and socialist) dynamic, and the atomised structure reinforces this partial political disintegration .... The different styles of the two halves seem to be making a comment on the nature of history, and to be suggesting that we can put the past into order (neat, theatrical form) and analyse it in terms of both class and gender cause and effect, but that we cannot do the same with the present[37].

In the end we have to assume that the play is open ended: two questions relating to feminist politics are raised, leaving the members of the audience to debate the issues for themselves. Churchill's debate is not prescribed. Expected 'norms' are challenged at every level: working methods, character, actor's role, dramatic structure and its relationship to political argument.

36. *op. cit.* Churchill. p.3.
37. *op. cit.* Wandor. pp.171-172.

John McGrath and 7:84

The meaning of the name of John McGrath's company gives a clue to the political nature of his theatre work. It relates to the statistic published in *The Economist* in 1966 that asserted that 7% of the population of this country owned 84% of the wealth. Although John McGrath is a playwright and screen writer, possibly more so than he is a director, his place within this survey of European theatre will lay emphasis on his theories of theatre and the role of his company. It is a misnomer to call the company *his*, for the emphasis here is on the collective endeavour, more so even than the two previously quoted theatre practitioners, Brenton and Churchill. The points of focus for this section will be the formation of *7:84* and a series of lectures given by John McGrath to a seminar in Cambridge University in 1979 and published by Methuen in 1981.

Much of what has passed for socialist theatre (or indeed working class theatre) in post-war Britain has had more to do with a reformist position that relates revolutionary ideas to an elevated form of art. This is particularly of note when dealing with the theatre that was emerging in Britain in the 1950s. The plays of John Osborne (*Look Back in Anger*) and Arnold Wesker (*Roots*) owe more in both their form and content to nineteenth-century Naturalism, than they do to Bertolt Brecht, or any of the revolutionary artists at work in the inter-war years of Europe. In a curious way the great experiments in art that occurred in the rest of Europe in the first half of this century, passed by Britain without much impact. This may well be seen as a part of Britain's self-absorption as it copes with the post–imperial period, or it may be put down to basic insularity, or both. The 'new' experiences being articulated by Osborne and Wesker employed what were essentially nineteenth-century dramatic narrative structures and were more to do with personal identity than they were concerned with the broader issues of revolutionary politics. Certainly Arnold Wesker would appear to have measured his art by the standards of bourgeois art.

> What is revolutionary art? Art whose forms are different from anything we've seen before ... or using bourgeois art forms to say revolutionary things? I've never encountered working class art ... I don't subscribe to the affected notions that music hall was art or that pop music is art ...[38]

John McGrath and his colleagues (such as Elizabeth MacLennan) argued strongly in favour of, not only a revolutionary form art, but also, as a way forward, the recognition of working class culture.

Not since the work of *Unity Theatre* in the 1930s and the employment of Brecht's concept of the *Lehrstücke* by the Communist party and the Labour party in the 1930s, had British theatre work been quite so significantly influenced by the theorists and practitioners in the rest of Europe. *7:84* was founded in England in 1971. In 1973, the company split in order that *7:84* Scotland and 7:84 England may be formed as separate companies; in 1985 the Arts

38. Quoted in MacLennan, E. *The Moon Belongs to Everyone: making theatre with 7:84*. London: Methuen. 1990, p.17.

Council subsidy was withdrawn from *7:84* England and, in spite of support from the Greater London Council (until its own demise) and the *TUC* it was, by 1986, without any obvious means of support.

Of interest in terms of theatrical structures is the *7:84* Scotland's touring production of *The Cheviot, the Stag and the Black, Black Oil* written by John McGrath. In particular, it is the form of the *ceilidh* (apart from the whole question of colonialism that relates it to the quoted work of Brenton and Churchill) that is of interest in relationship to McGrath's understanding of working class art. The *ceilidh* is a predominantly Gaelic communal art form that combines different strategies within the single event; elements of song, dance, and storytelling all combine together to produce an interactive relationship with an audience; the experience of the event is 'owned' by both performers and the audience.

In his book *A Good Night Out*, based on the series of lectures given at Cambridge University, McGrath pursues the argument for a working-class art structure that differs in its relationship to the audience, as much as in its structure, from the bourgeois art forms[39]. That is not to argue that working-class or popular art is intrinsically radical, or subversive. It is the system of meanings and the performer-audience relationships that offer the potentiality for a radical intervention in a given status quo. So called 'popular art' and so called 'high art' have an uneasy relationship with the former usually being relegated to a subversive role in a process that naturalises the values promulgated by 'high art'. Of course some 'popular art' ('populist'?) is reactionary and some 'high art' is potentially radical.

McGrath's aim is to find a theatre and a language that tells a story from a perspective different to that of bourgeois culture. His exploration commences with an account of the nature and structure often to be found in the style of entertainment offered by the British tradition of working-men's clubs, particularly in the north of England. The place is the Chorlton-cum-Hardy Club sometime in 1963. The initial description is forbidding, giving the overall impression of the utilitarianism of a 'nineteenth-century institution', with its often contradictory purposes in meeting the needs of the local community, while simultaneously exploiting them. The sign over the entrance declaring 'Members Only' Mcgrath sees as 'fair warning' in itself; presumably referring to the inherent sexism of such institutions, then and now[40]. The interior is described briefly as being large with a bar the length of one side of the room and a stage at one end. In the middle of the room is a small dance floor and a large wrestling ring. Tables occupy most of the space offering room for about four hundred people. The form of entertainment that McGrath then goes on to describe is a structure that comprises many differing elements that deny the expectation of a through linear narrative, demanding of the audience a wide range of responses that in many ways all contradictions of each other.

39. McGrath, J. *A Good Night Out: Popular Theatre: Audience, Class and Form*. London: Methuen. 1981.

40. *Ibid.* p.22.

He lists a representative menu of events that involves a Master of Ceremonies who plays the electric organ and also tells jokes. His task is to 'warm up' the audience. The evening then offers in succession:

> an up-and-coming comedian/crooner or young girl who bounces around singing pop songs merrily all teeth and tulle ... Ernie will come on, after a ten-to-fifteen minute act, and sing himself, or tell more stories ... then a group of young lads singing, not too loud, or another comic or vocalist or a ventriloquist ... then the moment you've all been waiting for, Ernie wheels on the bingo machine ...[41]

The events that follow all add to the general raising of the emotional and physical tension of the occasion. A wrestling bout, combined with the now increased consumption of alcohol, produces an increased level of excitement. This is followed by a stripper, more wrestling and, finally dancing to Ernie playing on the electronic organ. McGrath describes a scene of rising excitement and eventually violence as the combination of alcohol, visual and aural stimulation takes effect. 'Is this, then, working-class entertainment, the raw material of a future proletarian theatre?[42]' McGrath argues that it is not the only, nor the best, example of working-class entertainment; but that its brutality and sexism 'bears all the marks of the suffering of the urban industrial working class of the north of England[43]'. The elements that combine, in contradictory form, to provide the structure for this entertainment (the characteristics of song, music, communal dance, physical action, directness of presentation, addressing the audience in a conspiratorial manner, freedom of movement between performer and audience), are those elements that we may observe in popular art, often in revolutionary contexts.

We may relate this model of theatrical structure and the performer's relationship with the audience to the experience of nineteenth-century French cabaret in, for example the *Chat Noir* in the 1880s, or the *Blue Blouse Theatre Groups* that flourished between 1919 and 1928 in the Soviet Union. While it did not not strictly speaking occurr in revolutionary times, the *Chat Noir* started in 1881, just ten years after the Paris commune. Founded out of the *Hydropathes Society* by Roldolphe Salis, an evening at the *Chat Noir* would find the bourgeoisie of Paris travelling out to Montmartre to be confronted by an electic performance. Perhaps the significant difference between the *Chat Noir* and the Charton-cum-Hardy Working Men's Club was that the Montmartre audience was very deliberately abused by the performers. There is an amusing pun on the name of one of the major performers, Emile Goudeau, which relates back to the *Hydropathes Society*. It relates, if it can be put with a degree of delicacy, to Goudeau's name being translated as 'a taste of water' and the sexual perversion known as the 'amber rain'. The audience were, metaphorically pissed on, soundly abused, and they loved it! Perhaps the tenor of the occasion is best exemplified by lines one of Jules Jouy's popular songs at the *Chat Noir*.

41. *Ibid.* pp. 22-25.
42. *Ibid.* p.25
43. *Ibid.* p.27.

Patrons! tas d' Héliogabales,
D' effroi saisis

Quand vous tomberez sous nos balles
Chair à fusils,
Pour que chaque chien sur vos trognes
Pisse à l' écart.
Nous leur laisserons vos charognes ...[44]

Bosses, you Heliogabales,
You will be seized by fear

When you fall beneath our bullets,
Flesh for rifles,
Every dog will piss on your bloated faces
In solitary places.
We will leave them your carrion ...

McGrath's example of the *Blue Blouse Theatre Groups* is perhaps of even more direct relevance. He quotes a typical programme that any one of the groups might regularly perform. The items include: dramatic forms (including comic sketches); forms derived from dance and gymnastics; techniques derived from the plastic arts; and musical numbers. The point to be made is to do with concepts of narrative structure as much as it is a concern for radical content. McGrath argues that the 'leftist' radical dramas produced by the *Royal Court Theatre* throughout the 1950s, 1960s and 1970s, were still essentially bourgeois in both in form, content and audience; a narrative form with which the middle class audiences were both familiar and comfortable.

The disruption of clear narrative form has been at the centre of many of the most radical and innovative European theatre practitioners in the twentieth century. Apart from those figures and movements already mentioned, we may still observe the influence of Brecht, Piscator and Meyerhold. All of them by their various methods drew on forms of popular art as a means to disrupt the comfortable flow of the seamless narrative. This is not the cynical appropriation of naive forms of popular entertainment; indeed one might argue it is a return to the transient, 'less respectable' and subversive qualities, intrinsic to the majority of much western theatre activity that existed before the eighteenth century.

The clear example that may be quoted from the work of John McGrath is the play in *ceilidh* form, *The Cheviot, The Stag and The Black, Black Oil*. The subject matter is best described by McGrath himself in a long letter to the Scottish Arts Council, written when appealing against the decision not to fund *The Cheviot, The Stag and The Black, Black Oil*:

44. Title unknown, but quoted in Appignanesi, L. *Cabaret — The First Hundred Years*. New York: Grove Press. 1984, p.19.

> The play starts with the Clearances, goes for a quick look at the Red River to see what happened to those who went to Canada, then has a section on the Victorian romanticisation of the Highlands, Monarch of the Glen and all, moves on to look at those who settled in Glasgow, and then comes up-to-date with a sequence on the impact the oil is likely to have on the Highland way of life. It all sounds a bit of an epic, but it will be told in short scenes, with a lot of comedy, and music, and our own accordion band ... Wherever possible, i.e. almost everywhere, the play will be followed by a dance ...[45]

This is the form of popular art — that is a popular and traditional art form of the people who are the subject of the play — talking to/with people about their own history. The argument is that understanding your own history is the means by which you have the opportunity to control your own future. 'Passive acceptance now means losing control of the future'[46]. The structure has a good pedigree in popular theatre; it was the custom in the public theatres of London in the sixteenth and seventeenth centuries to end a performance (even that of a tragedy) with a jig. In the Elizabethan public theatre there was no need for the hard and fast definitions between 'high' and 'low' art; all was popular art. *7:84* danced with their audience.

It is obvious that the writers and directors discussed in relation to British theatre in the 1970s, represent but a small number of those people at work, and that they represent only a part of the ideological spectrum. However, the work represented bears a significant relationship to the development of post-war European consciousness. Each one (Brenton, Churchill and McGrath) exemplifies, in different ways, the complexity and dilemma of post-war Britain. Britain's seemingly uneasy identity as a part of Europe, in the concrete sense of the European Community, rests, in part, on the struggle for a new post-war identity in what is clearly the post-imperial phase for this country. The questions that surround ideas of personal and national identity have been addressed far more clearly by the 'alternative' sector of theatre practice in this country.

The large national companies, the West-end musicals, the variety compilations of pop songs sold as biographies of the 'star' and the endless revivals of old hits, are inextricably caught up with the marketing of a particular brand of culture. On the one hand, the national companies (the *RSC* etc.) see themselves as the producers of an art that ultimately is transcendent of material practice; the seamless narrative that deals in 'higher feelings'. However, there is also a culture that does not seek to transform, or enable its potential audience, but seeks to maximise its profitability. There is much research to be done in this field, particularly in the negotiations that are transacted internationally between production companies, within and outside Europe, on the packaging of theatre as a commodity. In its crudest sense, it is the resolve to preserve in every detail the factors that made 'X' show in London a financial success, so that it may be

45. *op. cit.* MacLennan. p.47.
46. McGrath, J. Introduction to *The Cheviot, The Stag and The Black, Black Oil.* West Highland Publishing Co. Ltd. 1974.

sold in the same way in Sydney or Brasilia, without regard to the intercultural complexities of such an activity. The industry that supports both these forms of cultural production — at least in the UK — ranges from the merchant banks and investors, through to the actors and musicians trade unions and the drama schools.

The generation of technicians, actors and musicians that have worked in the alternative theatres, possess a very different ideology of work (namely the collective) to those who have been trained through most of the drama and stage schools. The mainstream tradition demands exclusivity; the alternative tradition (which goes back to the 1920s, 1930s and 1940s) seeks a dialogue with its audiences. To paraphrase Walter Benjamin writing about Brecht's aim in the theatre, 'we should seek to think with feeling and feel thoughtfully'.

Eugenio Barba and the Odin Teatret

There is an approach to theatre that has drawn on the writings of Antonin Artaud; it developed in the 1960s and has come to prominence in the decades since. It is an approach that has sought, by concentrating on the actor, to develop theatre as an area of serious research — sometimes claiming a kind of quasi-scientific analysis — sometimes veering more towards the mystical. Often the primary aim has been more to focus on experimentation, aiming at the development of a vocal and physical sonority, than it has to present performance in conventional spaces and contexts. Many of the experimenters in this range of practice see themselves as reclaiming theatre from its subservient position in relationship to literature. By placing the actor at the centre of their concern, they see themselves re-asserting theatre, in its primary physicality, as an art in its own right, rather than as an interpretative craft.

There are many who work within this broad ideology, often in communities, demanding of their followers an almost monastic commitment and level of asceticism. They represent a significant strand in post-war European theatre, owing much to reconstructions of various practices in Indian and Japanese theatre (as we have observed in the work of Peter Brook). One such practitioner is Eugenio Barba, originally from Italy, but with much of his working life centred around his group, Odin Teatret, in Holstebro in Denmark. In locating Barba's contribution to the development of post-war European theatre it will be necessary to account for two aspects of his work: his concept of theatre anthropology and the actual theatrical practice as manifest through the theatre group that he founded.

Barba worked with the Polish director, Jerzy Grotowski for three years in his theatre 'laborator' and would claim that Grotowski was the single most important influence on his own work. Returning to western Europe and finding himself at odds with conventional theatrical thinking, Barba drew a group of young people around him (largely rejects from drama schools and theatres) and, in 1966, set up the group that was to become known as the *Odin Teatret*. Their place of work in Holstebro, Denmark was also their home. The analogy of a guru with his disciples leading a monastic communal existence would be accurate. Both Barba and Grotowski's work possesses that sense of commitment and determination (some would say obsessiveness) that requires their withdrawal from the normal traffic of life. And while claiming (on Barba's part) to be concerned with the demystification of theatre, there certainly runs the possibility of substituting one mystery for another.

It is necessary to start with Barba's definition of the term 'theatre anthropology'. His explanation seems to focus on an idea that, as we understand anthropology on a socio-cultural level, we must also understand it on a biological level. The context for this dual study is the moment of 'representation'. 'Theatre anthropology is thus the study of human beings' socio-cultural and physiological behaviour in a performance situation'[47]. Initially it seems that the experience of working with Grotowski in Poland has led Barba to focus his work on the performer; excluding from his research the visual, aural and, indeed, economic structures that many would argue are intrinsically a part of that moment of 'representation'.

However, in his own words his research began, not because of his interest in the actor *per se*, but in the 'oriental' theatre and its performers:

> My research began because of my interest in oriental theatre. I couldn't understand how oriental actors, even during a cold technical demonstration, nevertheless retain a very striking quality of presence which inevitably captures one's attention. In such a situation an actor is not interpreting or expressing anything. Yet he seems to radiate from a kernel of energy — evocative, knowledgeable, and yet unpremeditated — capturing our attention and magnetising our senses[48].

Barba argues that this not a question of skilled technique, but is a particular use of the body. He draws a distinction between what he terms, 'daily technique' and an 'extra-daily technique'. The daily technique of body movement is that which has been acquired by cultural conditioning, social status, and our professions. The extra-daily technique is, it is implied, transcendent of those socio-material conditions and is the result of a codified theatre. This codified theatre is present in oriental cultures, but not he argues, in the occidental theatre. The reason for this, he submits, is because the art of an actor does not exist in occidental theatre. 'There are modes and conventions, but anything arbitrary is possible under the domain of subjectivity, individualism, and lack of technical nomenclature and precise units of judgement'[49].

. The argument seems to be a stand against subjective individualism i.e. the individual's sensibility towards art as the ultimate yardstick for judgement, in favour of a more clearly codified cultural structure, wherein the individual is required to learn the

47. Barba, E and Savarese, N. *The Secret Art of the Performer*. London: Routledge.1991, p.8.
48. Barba, E. 'Theatre Anthropology in Action' in *Théâtre International*. No.1 International Theatre Institute. 1981, p.11.
49. *Ibid*. p.11.

codes that have been in place for generations. It is this latter process that, Barba argues, offers greater ultimate potential both for the performer and observer. The 'objectivity' provided by a codified culture ultimately offers greater freedom by creating the potential for a 'scientific' method of investigation to be employed in the analysis of the performer's energy manifest in the 'extra-daily' technique.

> The scientific method of investigation consists in choosing a field where the repetition of certain phenomena permits the disclosure of certain constants or 'laws'. If we choose oriental theatre as our field of investigation and analyse the oriental actor's utilisation of his body, we will immediately discover three 'laws'[50].

Barba expresses these three 'laws' as: (i) equilibrium, (ii) opposition and (iii) coherent incoherence. He quotes Japanese No and Kabuki theatre, Indian Orissi dance, Balinese acto-dancers and the western classical ballet as forms of codified theatre (classical western ballet he argues is the only example in occidental theatre). What they have in common, he argues, is that they all require a deformation of the daily technique of walking based on an alteration of equilibrium.

> By rejecting 'natural equilibrium', the oriental affects his environment by means of a 'de-lux equilibrium', uselessly complex, seemingly superfluous, and costing excess energy'[51].

Briefly, it seems that the purpose of this disequilibrium is to produce an intensification of certain organic processes and aspects of the body's life. We may presume that this means an altered state in the performer's body which signals her or him as 'other'. That the moment of representation is related to, but removed from the 'daily' world

The second 'law' that he quotes is 'opposition'. Again his reference point is the oriental theatre, in particular the Chinese theatre, though which Chinese theatre is not made clear. Here the theory is based on the observation that in Chinese theatre if an actor wishes to make a gesture in one direction, the actor starts by moving in the opposite direction. On the surface this would seem to indicate a useful ploy enabling the actor to surprise the observer. Secondly, no action is entirely predictable. Certainly this was a technique employed by the Soviet director Meyerhold, where he argued that all actions have a preparation, an action, and a recovery — the recovery inevitably being a preparation for the next action. Here, we may hazard the idea that Meyerhold was concerned with 'framing' an action — foregrounding its theatricality, in order that the action may be read as a part of broader social spectrum. Barba's analysis involves a complex — and to many people a seemingly quasi-scientific — analysis involving the bio-electrical discharge resulting from muscular activity. No real reason is given for this phenomenon, other than to say that in the oriental theatre, movements are complex, involving a curved trajectory.

50. *Ibid.* p.12.
51. *Ibid.* p.13.

Barba defines the third law as 'coherent incoherence'. This 'law' is based on the notion that it is incoherent for the actor to hamper an action by assuming positions which restrict the progress of the action. The reason given is that the actor can transform this seeming incoherence into, 'a new culture of the body through practice and training and by a process of enervation and the development of new nervomuscular reflexes. The extra-daily technique thus created becomes extremely coherent'[52].

It is the role of biological processes by which the actor may attain a different potential for physical action, and by which a strengthened physical presence is achieved before any form of personal (psychological?) reaction is set in motion. On one level Barba's work would seem to be in the European twentieth-century tradition of movements that have rejected the psychological behaviourism of nineteenth-century Naturalism, seeking in many different forms to establish the moment of representation as 'other' to the objective reality of daily life. However, Barba's intention is to be 'scientific' in his analysis of the means by which the 'otherness' of the performer is understood.

What Barba does not seem to take into account are the material cultural conditions that produced the theatrical forms that he observes in oriental theatre. The codes and laws that he cites are, by and large, taken out of any discernible context, with the assumption that they are universal and may be transposed into western European cultures (the occident). While declaring that he wishes, by his 'scientific' methodology, to demystify theatrical practice, he stands ironically in grave danger of mystifying what is open and understood in its original context. The transposition (appropriation) of other cultural methods and codes is often seen as creating an avant garde in the host culture; an avant garde that by its own definition is ahead, and therefore, apart from the popular movements of that culture. It is interesting that ten years after the original hypothesis was postulated, Barba, in 1991, published further thoughts on the definition of theatre anthropology. His ideas regarding laws seem to have been modified to a degree.

> Different performers, at different places and times and in spite of the stylistic forms specific to their traditions; have shared common principles. The first task of theatre anthropology is to trace theses recurrent principles. They are not proof of the existence of a 'science of the theatre' nor of a few 'universal laws'. They are nothing more than particularly good bits of advice; information useful for scenic practice. To speak of a 'bit of good advice' seems to indicate something of little value when compared with the expression 'theatre anthropology'. But entire fields of study — rhetoric and morals, for example, or the study of behaviour — are likewise collections of 'good advice'[53].

While Barba has attained a reputation as a theatre pedagogue/researcher, he is, of course, as well regarded for the work

52. *Ibid.* p.17.
53. *op. cit.* Barba and Savarese. p.8.

of his theatre group *Odin Teatret*. The research work is intrinsically a part of the theatre-making objectives of the group, necessitating long periods, often up to a year, of research/rehearsal. In the late 1970s the *Odin Teatret* underwent a change in the direction of their work, emphasising interaction with communities, rather than more conventional performance work in dedicated spaces. Initially they installed themselves in a small village in southern Italy with the intention of working with and for that community. The result was open air theatre utilising a wide range of skills drawn from the circus and music. Quite what it did for the economically impoverished village community in southern Italy is difficult to ascertain. In August 1980 *Odin Teatret* took up a residency in Wales. This project is more clearly documented. It took the form of three phases. The first involved being located in the capital Cardiff working closely with the *Centre For Performance Research*, which is an independent theatre organisation dedicated to facilitating research in performance, as well as organising tours, arranging conferences and housing a multi-cultural library and reference centre. This first phase consisted of performances, demonstrations and workshops.

The second phase involved the company travelling out to three towns in Wales with the intention of performing selected works, but perhaps of more importance, the exchange of ideas and practices. The third phase involved drawing other individuals and groups into the project and, working with the different communities around Wales, preparing performance pieces for those particular communities. The whole project returned to Cardiff where all the different groups shared the results of their work.

It is clear that whatever form of critique may be raised in regard of work ideology, the *Odin Teatret* with Eugenio Barba is a part of the movement that sees itself as a part of a serious alternative to mainstream theatres. The movement out of theatres (and away from traditional European training methods, as exemplified by many of the drama schools), represents a desire to see in theatre an enabling role, more than its role of commodity production. Questions still need to be raised regarding the exact nature of the activity when theatre companies move into small and often economically impoverished communities. The questions relate to the nature of the relationship between cultures and their often differing status. The carnivalesque quality of the events raises questions in itself. Is it a force for subversion and liberation, or is it more likely to be (and one could argue this as its traditional function) a force for repression. The paradigm of *Mardi Gras* and Lent is the obvious example — carnival as the safety valve for the established political status quo.

There are many such experiments being pursued throughout Europe, though fewer now in Britain, with the increasing withdrawal of government subsidy from alternative approaches to theatre, in favour of the more mainstream production of high commodity art. It is worth mentioning the British based group *Welfare State International*. They were founded in 1968 and, like many other such groups and individuals, were informed, ideologically, by the regrouping of political/cultural activity in the late 1960s. It was, and still is, a multi-media company that is eclectic, not only in its materials and methods, but also in its wide embrace of differing ideologies. In many ways *Welfare State International* seems to embody the 'impurity' of form that has always been the hallmark of popular art.

The material resources of *Welfare State International* are many and certainly within the reach of most people: 'sculptures using found materials (as well as fire and ice), puppetry, landscape, food, fireworks, technology, dance, performance and weather'[54]. Their skills range from theatre-making in its more readily recognisable forms, to the devising of rituals for particular communities or groups in a society that exists in 'a mythological near-vacuum'. Baz Kershaw in his book, *Engineers of the Imagination* brings a theoretical perspective to the work, by highlighting the complexity of the simultaneous contradictions at work in the company. It is the series of paradoxes embodied by the company, that makes its work possess the potential not only to exist in an increasingly hostile world, but to provide moments for theatre (in its broadest sense) to create substantial locations for radical intervention in the political/cultural status quo.

> At the heart of the *Welfare State* project rests a series of paradoxes that inform every aspect of the company's ever changing practice ... these paradoxes are the foundation for the irony and the humour which continually connect the work to a spirit of resistance that aims to change the world ... the paradoxes are the product of the company's increasingly determined attempt to mount a socio-politically critical practice in an ideologically hostile environment[55].

It would seem, from the evidence of the last few examples quoted in this section, that we can no longer rely on the certainty of theatrical practices in Europe to remain enclosed within their physical and cultural structures. Art, in a variety of ideological forms, is moving out to connect directly with the audience with which it wishes to engage. Clearly though, there are dangers. The relationship, whatever it may be, between performers and audience is one of exchange. The exchange may be perceived on two related levels: that of commodity exchange — the performance as fixed commodity in exchange for payment; or it may be an ideological exchange between performers and audience. This is not to say that at the former level the exchange is not an also an ideological exchange, but that in the former example the fixed nature of the art commodity leaves little room for negotiation. Useful terms to describe the different forms of exchange may be termed 'closed cultural event' and 'open cultural event'.

Theodor Adorno of the Frankfurt School raises questions relating to this problem of exchange. He develops Marx's argument that commodity exchange effects an equation between things that are in fact incommensurable to argue that ideological thought also effects

54. Coult, T and Kershaw, B. eds. *Engineers of the Imagination*. London: Methuen. 1990, p.1.
55. *Ibid*. p.200.

just such an equation[56]. His analysis suggests that ideological thought
is revolted by the sight of 'otherness' which is either outside of its
own closed system, or threatens to escape it, that it violently reduces
it to its own image and likeness. Ideology for Adorno, as Terry
Eagleton suggests, is a form of 'identity thinking': that 'identity is the
primal form of all ideology'[57].

How then does this line of analysis relate to the practices that we
have observed in the last section. What questions does the nature of
ideological exchange raise when we consider the various kinds of
appropriations being made by Peter Brook or Eugenio Barba in
relationship to what they broadly term oriental theatre? What is the
nature of the exchange between Brenton and his audience at the
National Theatre and John McGrath in a village hall in the
Highlands of Scotland? These are questions that interrelate the
ideological exchange (appropriation) with commodity exchange.

Ariane Mnouchkine and the *Théâtre du Soleil*
The *Théâtre du Soleil* was organised as a collective before the political
demonstrations of 1968. This is an important point to bear in mind
before entering a discussion of this particular development in
European theatre. For while the *Théâtre du Soleil* bears many of the
hallmarks of the collective radicalism of post late 1960s theatre, close
scrutiny reveals many curious anomalies that relate the work of the
Théâtre du Soleil to the exotic and individualistic modes of practice
discerned in the lineage of Brook, Grotowski and Barba. Ariane
Mnouchkine founded the company and has certainly been, and still
is at the age of sixty one, its *éminence*. Her background is European.
She studied at both the universities of Paris and Oxford and she
travelled widely, particularly to Asia, returning to found the *Théâtre
du Soleil* with the intention of researching into the possibilities of a
'people's theatre'.

The company from the very start was created as a worker's co-
operative which comprised about ten performers, designers and
technicians, all of whom had equal salaries and voting rights. Lenora
Champagne in her study of French theatre around the events of
1968 informs us that, from 1967, the company received a variety of
grants and subsidies from the Ministry of Cultural Affairs.

> However, the subsidies are usually inadequate for the company's
> needs and the troupe's debts usually exceed its income, forcing the
> members of the collective to depend on unemployment benefits to
> seek outside jobs[58].

This was probably the case in the late 1960s, but according to John
Allen, the *Théâtre du Soleil* is one of the few companies — certainly
from the 1980s onwards — that could survive on its box office
receipts, such is the popularity of its work.

The first stage of the company's work was text based (latterly
there has been a return to this mode of work) with the consequence
that the idea of a practice based on the concept of collectivity was

56. Commodity exchange is effected by the agreement that two entirely different commodities, for example, a book and 30 litres of petrol, have exchange value, because there is an agreement that it took the same amount of labour power to produce them. The specific differences between these objects is suppressed, as their use-value becomes subordinate to their abstract equivalence.

57. Eagleton, T. *Ideology*. London: Verso. 1991, pp.125-158.

58. Champagne, L. *French Theatre Experiment Since 1968*. UMI Research Press. 1984. Chapter 3, footnote p.27.

inevitably restricted to the social and economic structure of the company. The creative theatre-making was still based on an ideology that maintained traditional working practices (at least in the modern tradition that had evolved from the artistic status quo established by the *Meiningen Company* in the 1830s)[59]. The two notable productions from the period between 1964 and 1968 were single authored texts, Arnold Wesker's *The Kitchen* and Shakespeare's *A Midsummer Night's Dream*.

According to Lenora Champagne's account, during the May demonstrations of 1968 the *Théâtre du Soleil* stopped performances of *A Midsummer Night's Dream* and commenced a series of performances of *The Kitchen* in factories occupied by workers. This was as an expression of solidarity with the striking workers and marked for the company a significant change of direction in the nature of their theatre work. As a result of their demonstration with the workers and students, they were expelled from the *Cirque Medrano*, the Parisian theatre where they had been working. This necessitated not only a change in their site of work, but also a re-assessment of their whole approach to theatre. The ideology of collectivism that had marked the social and economic structure of the company, was now extended to their methodology of theatre-making. From now on, their new approach demanded that they rejected the prescribed text and worked collectively on devised theatre that arose from improvisation and debate. This approach to theatre-making has been copied by many small companies all over Europe, but none really with the skill and commitment demanded by Ariane Mnouchkine. This observation points to a series of interesting contradictions in the work of Mnouchkine and her company, for while the radical change due to the events of 1968 deserve recording, the exact nature of the company's radicalism demands scrutiny. This is not in any sense meant as a test of some notion of political purity, but more in search of the curious ways by which we are defined by culture, and the ways by which we define our cultures.

A significant feature of the *création collective* was that practical training became a central issue in the company's work. It is also a way for Mnouchkine to gain new actors for the company. So many of the drama schools in Europe are, to an extent by necessity, preoccupied with training men and women for the mainstream theatre as it exists; their approach has to be essentially pragmatic. A by-product of this approach is that the status quo for women is heavily weighted against them. By and large, the essentially reactionary attitude of the men who run drama schools, sees the task as being one of providing actors for a theatre where there are not many parts for women. Outside of this mainstream theatre — hopefully as it has become clear in this volume — an alternative theatre in many different forms has evolved. For Mnouchkine, as for many others, the preferred route is the educating of their own actors — perhaps for a theatre that they would like to see in the future,

59. The 'modern' concept of the director is derived, it is commonly accepted, from the court company established by George II, the Duke of Sax-Meiningen with his stage-manager/director, Ludwig Chronegk.

rather than meeting the needs of supply and demand.

Mnouchkine holds an annual open workshop at the *Théâtre du Soleil's Cartoucherie* in the suburbs of Paris. These workshops are rarely advertised in any formal sense, but regularly there may be a thousand people from all over the world wanting to seek admission. Individuals are interviewed and about two hundred admitted. Mnouchkine's attitude is dictatorial, and perhaps she has every right to be so, for the workshops are free of charge. Josette Féral who teaches at the University of Quebec attended one of these workshops in the early 1980s and recorded the events in *The Drama Review*[60]. There do not seem to be any of the conventional trappings of the drama workshop: no voice class, no movement classes. What is there, is an intensive series of improvisations using masks and costumes. Mnouchkine makes it quite clear that an apprenticeship involves *looking* as much as acting. Students (referred to as trainees) work on improvisations and present them in turn for the scrutiny of Mnouchkine. She demands attention from everyone at all times and her criticism of what the trainees do is important for everyone in the room, not just the people whose work to which she is attending.

She appears to be like Barba and Brook in the discipline and attentiveness she demands. But she does seem to differ in her primary use of mask and costume. Not for Mnouchkine the bare stage and the actor stripped naked.

> I would like to remind everyone that this is a workshop. Seven days we will share together. It is not an audition. If you come to the carpet to show yourself, or to show Me, you will not be showing anything. It is not a training to prove yourself. It is a training for the theatre[61].

There are two elements here to be noted: the demand that watching, and presumably listening, are as important as action in the learning process; and that the extra-human dimensions of mask and costume are integral to her ideas of theatricality. It appears that she differs from the other European 'masters' (mensch?) in these two very fundamental points.

Other theatre practitioners in this 'alternative' field of activity tend towards the denial of the extra dimensions of mask and costume, at least in the training period. Mnouchkine, however, draws on a tradition of European popular theatre, in particular the *commedia dell'arte*. Her work gives pre-eminence to the mask as a source for the trainee's initial creative work. She also has a special use for costumes, in both training and performance, that indicates a sensual quality to her theatre. This seems appropriate to the theatre that she creates — a theatre that while spectacular is not epic, at least not in the way that Brecht used the concept historically. Mnouchkine's theatre is sensual in its sense of a panorama of human activity occurring simultaneously. There was a similar effect in Howard Brenton's *Epsom Downs*. This play depicts one day in the life of the hordes of people who pour out of London for Derby day. Brenton

60. *The Drama Review*: a journal of performance studies. Schechner, R. ed. MIT Press. 1989. Vol. 33 No. 4.

61. Féral, J. 'Mnouchkine's Workshop at the Soleil' in *The Drama Review*. 1989. p.79. The 'carpet' is the demarked area of floor space set aside for the showing of improvisations.

denies that the play is epic in Brecht's use of the term; for Brecht, epic signals a dialectical collage of small lives in conjunction with the moment of monumental history. Much of Mnouchkine's earlier work creates a similar kaleidoscopic effect, creating myriad images that are sensual, but lacking the potentiality of a more dialectical structure. Perhaps a more accurate description would be, as Lenora Champagne quotes Alfred Simon, that the work tends towards mythologisation of events, more than towards a materialist historical analysis[62].

Much of the new European tradition of post-war alternative theatre seems, at least to the outside observer, to eschew the rational and intellectual analysis, in favour of a more subjective opening of the actor to 'irrational' sensation. Despite the claim to a scientific analysis of energy in the performed action, this would seem to be clearly exemplified by the work of Barba. Exceptions to this approach do exist and the *Joint Stock Theatre Company*'s collective approach to theatre-making often required endless hours of discussion, both about the creative process, as well as the social structure of the group. Mnouchkine's working practices demand that discussion around the practice in hand is an integral part of the collective creative process. Apart from the recognition of observation and discussion as a physical activity (a point missed by many theatre practitioners when arguing their cause against the theoretician), the act of discussion is an empowerment of the actor. In the training sessions the relationship is built on the level of interrogation, with Mnouchkine observing and demanding that the performers justify, both through discussion and performance, their narrative in the improvisation. Mnouchkine's role as director has become that of 'the first spectator'.

> Mnouchkine's (role) became largely one of watching the improvisations and making comments or suggestions as to the clarity, directness, and efficacy of the physical language. The improvisations were elaborated by the performer from there. This resulted in a give-and-take or dialogue process between the performers and the director and constituted a preliminary attempt at collective   problem solving ... each member explored his own creativity, leading to a new democracy in theatre, where actors could become 'authors as well as interpreters'[63].

The empowerment of the actor in this way is not, of course an isolated event. A good deal of critical theory, particularly in France, has been concerned with very fundamental questions relating to the nature of authorship. In particular we may make reference to Roland Barthes, *The Death of the Author* (1977) and Michel Foucault, *What is an Author?* (1969). While questions raised regarding the location and identity of authorship in the literary artefact may not be strictly analogous to theatre, there are certain appropriate considerations. They are not strictly analogous only in the sense that theatre goes through many stages in the process beyond the literary text — through theatrical script, to performance as text. The matter,

62. *op. cit.* Champagne. p.41.
63. *op. cit.* Champagne. p.35.

however, becomes even more interesting when, as Mnouchkine and the *Théâtre du Soleil* practise, theatre practitioners work collectively from their own devising of a 'theatrical text' through improvisation. It is clear that Mnouchkine's actors are collaborators in the construction of the theatrical event. Of course where Barthes and Foucault may come into the discourse is at the point of the performance. Then questions may be raised regarding the 'reading of the performance' by the audience, as an act of authorship in itself.

The period post the 1968 demonstrations has revealed the *Théâtre du Soleil* as a company with work ranging wide in its content and form. Between 1970 and 1977, apart from developing their own collectively created pieces they also devised and performed agit-prop street theatre pieces, often in response to particular requests. The two major theatrical presentations that the company has become known by are the *création collective* works based on the French revolution, *1789* and *1793: The Revolutionary City is of the World*. *1789* dealt with the social relationships and dynamics that created the French Revolution as the foundation for the growth of French bourgeois capitalism. *1793* dealt more with the question and reflections on the *sans culottes*. For a thorough critical analysis of this work and, in particular its relationship to 1968 reference should be made to Champagne's *French Theatre Experiment Since 1968*. The student of theatre may find reference back to Peter Weiss' text, *Marat/Sade* a useful exercise — especially if the focus is on the original reading of the play, rather than on Brooke's *Artaudian* reconstruction.

The Author and the Performance Text

Much of the discussion in this chapter has been concerned with the actor's break with the authored text. This, as may be seen with aspects of Mnouchkine's work, is a form of empowerment to the actor, allowing her or him to contribute to the making of theatre on a level more than that of interpretative crafts person. It is dangerous to reduce the history of theatre to clear cut trends, but while recognising a possible oversimplification, we may also observe the general impetus prior to this collective empowerment of the actor, as the period that established the status of the polemical director.

Inevitably, it is understandable that the writer should feel, by this empowerment of those that hitherto had been the servants of the text, a certain sense of being disenfranchised. At the present time, in the United States of America, there is a current spate of litigation involving playwrights suing theatre directors for the mis-representation of their texts. Since the inception of the director as a significant player in the theatrical game, there has existed a tension between the writer and those whose task it is to give action to the word. Now it would seem, that in the Western world, with the 'flowering' of late capitalism and the free market, that the real question of art as property is being institutionalised in the fullest legal sense.

In December 1980 the Budapest Playwrights' Conference met to discuss a number of issues relating to the position of playwrights in the contemporary European theatre. The main issue of the conference was the relationship between the playwright and the director. A manifesto was produced that made clear the degree of distress and disempowerment felt by playwrights. David Edgar, the British playwright reported in *Théâtre International* on the controversy:

> I think the argument over the *Playwrights' Manifesto* was particularly significant for the British and American delegations, because it brought home the depths of feeling that exist among European Playwrights about how their work is mangled by directors, and, indeed, their resentment at the way in which directors have become cinema-style 'superstars' over recent years[64].

Edgar goes on to record other matters of concern in the theatre relating to the broader issues of writing and the funding of theatre. These issues concern the amount of new plays being performed, and that subsidies for theatres should be related to a degree of commitment to new writing and the question of royalties (or lack of them) payable on long dead playwrights.

> Behind this manifesto lay the other document: a detailed and considered summary of the reforms necessary to preserve the original contemporary play as the mainspring of the theatre.

The most 'elegant' reform (as Edgar describes it) related to the idea that royalties should be payable on out-of-copyright playwrights and that the money be used to fund new work. The proposal removes the financial incentive to produce the work of the dead and provides money to finance the work of the living. The *Playwrights' Manifesto* is an important document and well deserving of being reproduced in full. The references to the playwright as being exclusively male are those of the *Playwrights' Manifesto* and not those of the author of this volume.

The Playwrights' Manifesto

> It is certainly an inventive production. Signor Visconti has invented a play, where major significant and quite crucial pieces of action are introduced into a play by the director, without consultation with the author. Let me remind you that a play is not public property. It belongs to its author[65].

Playwrights all over the world are angry. Something is wrong in the theatre. At first each one, solitary in his room, thought it was only happening to him. Now through *ITI* meetings, they have discovered one another and see they have problems in common. These are:

• the playwright feels an outsider to the institutions of which he is the life blood;

• classical plays predominate to the detriment of new contemporary ones, frequently in productions pursuing perverse artistic whims;

• when the new play is accepted it is often misinterpreted, altered,

64. *Théâtre International.* No.1, 1981.
65. Pinter, H. Commenting on Visconti's production of *Old Times* at the Teatro di Roma, 1973.

even mutilated in pursuit of an external artistic vision, or ephemeral fads;

• and finally, because it may take a minimum of a year to prepare and write a play which may then be presented for only a few weeks, the playwright is constantly in a precarious financial state.

Many feel the director's power can become a tyranny, stifling and inhibiting original, creative work. The director's profession is only a century old, the result of stage managers rising above themselves, as it were. Partly because of the imbalance between new and classical work, playwrights feel the director has achieved a position of power in the theatre that sometimes works against their interest. The living playwright is somewhat disconcerted to find himself undercut and pushed aside by his dead predecessors.

Further, the diminishing importance of the work as the mainspring of dramatic narrative is disturbing. Some theatres have decided that they can dispense with the playwright altogether and make theatre through improvisation or collective writing. But the word carries thought, and without it the theatre is threatened with the plight of the dinosaur whose body grew out of all proportion to the capacity of its brain.

So, solutions have been tentatively offered and discussed and certain aims have been formulated. The following has become clear:

• that an international organisation of playwrights is urgently needed to protect their interests, restore their prestige within the profession, defend the integrity of their work, and enable a sharing of experiences and solutions to flow between countries;

• that no theatre should receive subsidy unless it presents a larger proportion of new plays than is at present in evidence;

• that payment of writers in state-subsidised theatres should reflect a percentage of the real cost of the subsidised seat, not the low price at which it is offered to the public;

• that training and encouragement of the playwright should be in the direction of a new generation of playwright/directors, who run their own theatrical ensembles;

• that classical plays should be paid for, and the royalties earned by 'out-of-copyright' dramatists should go towards encouraging the work of their living colleagues.

In the delicate ecological balance of the theatre the work of the playwright constitutes a vital link whose gradual erosion or sudden destruction would threaten the entire theatrical structure. Of course, playwrights write for the theatre because they believe that collaboration between the arts of the writer, director, actor, and designer can create a unique emotional and intellectual experience for an audience. But they are convinced that the living word and the living writer of that word is and will remain the primary mainspring of the theatre.

We declare the playwright an endangered species!

In many senses there is no single answer to this question; at least there is not one answer that would meet the apparent needs of all those concerned with the making of theatre. The history of dramaturgy in Europe is a complex subject and the many different positions and status held by the maker of the dramatic text has undergone many transformations. The etymology of the word playwright, as opposed to the possible 'playwrite', is significant in itself, especially if we consider the ways by which a script was often achieved in the Elizabethan public playhouse. In that context it was the exception, rather than the rule, that a text was produced (wrought) by a single author.

There is a temptation to see the angst expressed in the manifesto as being bred out of the dominance held by the literary object, over the social art form, since the early nineteenth century. That is, with the rise of bourgeois individualism, came the pre-eminence of the literary novelistic form (something that one reads alone and in one's own time) over the collective social art, as represented by theatre certainly from the fifteenth century to the nineteenth century. It is quite clear that, for a variety of reasons, there has been a movement in post-war European theatre, back towards its more social and collective identity, and away from the individualistic dominance of the literary form. The economic factors that played a significant part in the rise of the novel as a pre-eminent literary form were matched by the emergence of twentieth-century literary theory and the establishing of literature as an academic discipline in universities. In the United Kingdom, the first Chair of English Literature was established at the University of Oxford, around the turn of the century, with Walter Raleigh (later to become Sir Walter Raleigh, though not sharing the same fate as his eminent namesake) being afforded the title of Professor of English Literature.

In part, it may be fair to argue that the history of this 'new' discipline has established a hegemony by which the study of the novel and poetry as 'literary' forms has absorbed the drama into themselves as a form of prose or poetry (depending on the nature of the dramatic language) and by this absorbing, marginalised the theatricality of dramatic form. The final chapter of this volume will attempt an analysis of the current re-emergence of nationalism in Europe. Is that ideology of property, individualism and nationalism that far removed from the ideology of the text as property, as expressed in the American need to prove it in court?

As a final stage in this chapter I would like to consider two playwrights and their close association with particular theatre companies. The two playwrights are Brian Friel and *The Field Day Theatre Company* and Howard Barker and *The Wrestling School*. The relationship of text to performance is an important issue and forms part of the pattern of cultural consciousness in contemporary European culture. However, there is another significant factor involved in considering both of these writers. While many countries that form the European Community have not been included in this brief survey, and nor have contemporary women writers been given the space that their significance demands, there is a substantial reason why Brian Friel should be considered — a reason not directly connected with his plays in isolation. The focus is the question of national identity, rather than the man. Likewise, Howard Barker is considered more on the level of the writer and a theatre group, than the writer as individual. This is not a lack of regard for these two writers, no more than I have a disregard for certain countries, or for women writers. The brief for this study is, albeit a broad survey, to indicate areas of work that are significant in that they locate and elucidate the workings and complexity of post-war European culture.

Brian Friel and *The Field Day Theatre Company*
The question of Irish identity is a complicated one and not always easy to appreciate from the outside. An analysis offered by Seamus Deane, one of *The Field Day Theatre Company* directors, centres on the idea that Ireland is a post-colonial country and that the violence in Northern Ireland is a 'lingering effect' of colonial rule[66]. The question of Europe's identity, as has already been suggested, is related to its own role as a post-colonial power. The evidence for this is seen as much in the work of people like Barba and Brook, as it is in the larger issues of Europe's political and economic relationships with the 'third world'. We have a situation where the two Irelands, constituent state(s) of the European Community are in themselves post colonial countries of another member European state. The matter is further complicated by the fact that one Ireland is a sovereign state in its own right (the Republic of Ireland) and the other Ireland (Northern Ireland) occupies (or some might argue is occupied) an ambiguous position in 'union' with Great Britain.

   The Field Day Theatre Company was founded in 1980 and is based in Derry in the north-west of Ireland (in the political entity, Northern Ireland). The playwright Brian Friel and the actor Stephen Rea were the founding members and have had as their guiding principle the concern with the relationship 'between myth and present-day perception, history and politics'[67]. *The Field Day Theatre Company* was very much an ad hoc affair set up, in the first instance, to produce Brian Friel's play *Translations* which, it was intended, would tour Ireland, but as a voice of Northern Ireland that transcended the sectarian divisions. As it was, the whole affair became something of much greater significance in terms of the cultural politics of Ireland, than anyone had envisaged.

   Marilynn Richtarik in *Acting Between the Lines* points out the significance of the city of Derry as the sight of this the first theatrical production under the aegis of *The Field Day Theatre Company*. Derry

66. Deane, S. ed. Introduction to *Nationalism, Colonialism and Literature*. Derry: Field Day. 1990.

67. Richtarik, M. J. *Acting Between the Lines, The Field Day Theatre Company and Irish Cultural Politics 1980-1984*. Oxford: Clarendon. 1994. p.10.

(to the Republicans) or Londonderry (to the Unionists) is a city that has enormous significance to both the Protestant and the Roman Catholic communities. For the Unionist faction, Londonderry is the symbol, through the stand against the siege of James II in 1689, of their determination to remain British. For the Republican faction, Derry stands out as the most blatant abuse of Protestant power against (what is in the city, though not in the province) a Catholic majority. Curiously, although the city of Derry became one of the major 'sparking' points for the current troubles it has, paradoxically, also been the one significant site of potential co-operation between the two communities.

The city, although the second city of Northern Ireland, has a history of neglect. In the early 1960s, in the face of industrial closure and rising unemployment, it had an opportunity to raise both its economic and its cultural prospects. The Derry communities united in a bid to create a second university (after Queen's Belfast) in the province. Despite overwhelming support within the city, from both communities, the placing of a second university went to staunchly Unionist Coleraine. This bid for a university, which of course would have brought employment to the city, failed because of the nature of Unionist politics in the rest of the province. The end result was that the two communities of Derry, who had achieved a degree of unity in their common bid, were once more thrown back into division and dissension. Richtarik argues, persuasively, that the ultimate tragedy of this increased sense of isolation and neglect was the event of Bloody Sunday on 30 January 1972.

The production of *Translations* opened in the Assembly Hall of the Guildhall in Derry:

> This building had been the favoured target of the IRA precisely because it had symbolised so well the Unionist domination of the city. When *Translations* opened on 23 September, the Guildhall was barricaded against further terrorist attacks and was still covered in scaffolding used by workmen to repair damage done by the last bombers. An exquisite touch of irony, which did not go unremarked at the time ... But if it was a symbol the Guildhall was a multi-faceted one. In 1980 it represented not only a corrupt past, but a more hopeful present and future. The new power-sharing Council which had replaced the Londonderry Corporation was finally giving the Catholic minority a meaningful voice in civic affairs, and councillors were anxious to promote culture and peaceful pursuits in the city[68].

It may be argued that this production of *Translations* had a political and cultural significance way beyond itself. The production toured Ireland, performing in village and school halls as often as it did in purpose built theatres. The play itself, centring around events in the 1830s when the English, as a part of colonisation process, translated the place names of Ireland into English, marked the end of Gaelic Ireland. Friel is concerned with language in the play and what it

68. *Ibid.* p.23.

means. The displacement of one language by another and of one culture by another, becomes the metaphor by which the alienation the Irish have felt, due to the English colonisation, is manifest. This production marked the beginning of a process whereby Ireland, and in particular Northern Ireland, began reasserting its own identity. *The Field Day Theatre Company* is determinedly and deliberately parochial in that it is of itself, and not measuring itself, in a provincial sense, against the metropolitan centres[69].

Out of the work of *The Field Day Theatre Company* has arisen a sense that art can be, in the poet Seamus Heaney's view, a determining factor in changing the political condition of a society. Marilyn Richtarik argues in her introduction to *Acting Between the Lines*, that the generation of people who founded *The Field Day Company* reached political awareness in the early 1960s, but throughout the 1970s and 1980s gradually lost confidence in political action, after the hopes of the civil rights movement disintegrated into deeply rooted sectarian violence. A new sense of the potential political efficacy of culture arose. This was based on the idea that it was necessary to change people's fundamental attitudes, before there could be a hope of substantial political change. Richtarik quotes Seamus Heaney on the matter:

> It can eventually make new feelings, or feelings about feelings
> happen, and anybody can see that in this country for a long time to
> come a refinement of feelings will be more urgent than a re-framing
> of policies or of constitutions[70].

I have considered *The Playwrights' Manifesto* in relation to the work of Brian Friel and the *Field Day Theatre Company*, in order that the reader may raise certain questions in the light of the *Manifesto* and one particular theatre practice. The collaboration that Friel has achieved since the founding of *The Field Day Theatre Company* (the company has now extended its interests to include poets as well as dramatists, directors and actors), and the degree to which the company is a part of cultural regeneration of a society, seems to deny the negativism that is the very keynote of *The Playwrights' Manifesto*.

Howard Barker and The Wrestling School

The Playwrights' Manifesto lays great emphasis on the centrality of the word in theatre. And, certainly with Brian Friel, that centrality has found a way to work collaboratively with the other elements that comprise the theatrical experience. In *Translations* the word as national/cultural identity was the central issue; the theatrical moment brought together both the word and the action, but it also brought together the communities through the word of theatre.

Howard Barker is also a playwright whose concern with the function of the word forms the major part of his craft. This is not to state the obvious; a playwright is one whose ideas are 'wrought' in words, but there are some whose concern to create a stage picture

69. *Ibid.* p.11.
70. Heaney, S. 'Editor's Note' in *Soundings '72.* Belfast. 1972. Quoted in Richtarik, M. 1994. p.6.

may give equal credence to the musical or the visual moment. The case with Barker is that words are central in a more exclusive sense.

Barker is of the same generation of playwrights as Howard Brenton, Caryl Churchill, David Hare and David Edgar, all of whom share the same concern for the debate that has arisen out of the post-war, post-colonial phase of British and European culture. While it would be naive to argue the similarities of these writers too closely, Barker does differ in a number of ways from the general ideological thrust of the others in that generation of writers. For many critics Barker has been a neglected figure when compared to the others of his generation, but there is more to the argument than that material condition. It may be argued that Barker's, 'interest in the psychopathology of capitalism and patriarchy leads him to deal in much of his work with the grotesque and the distorted, often in highly scatological language'[71].

Barker, while politically of the radical left, doesn't share with many of his generation a support for the various manifestations of popular art. His opposition to the power and conservatism exemplified by Thatcherism and its aftermath, includes a deep suspicion of mass culture and its social function. This suspicion is founded on the observation that the political right in Britain is profoundly suspicious of intellectuals and will exploit populist art as a distraction for the main body of the population. He will however, occasionally exploit the imagery of populist culture as a critique of the ideological philistinism that he perceives in right wing cynical cultural manipulation[72].

In March 1988, a group of actors announced that they were to form a company entirely devoted to the perform of the work of one playwright. The company is called *The Wrestling School* and the playwright, Howard Barker[73]. This is an unusual event by anyone's standard. Even the large 'national' companies, having their central focus in Shakespeare or Molière, include in their repertoires works by other playwrights. While this level of devotion to one playwright by a group of actors could be interpreted as a response to the relative neglect of Barker's work in the 1970s, it is equally an interesting riposte to the sense of alienation expressed by the signatories to *The Playwrights' Manifesto*.

The actor Ian McDiarmid stated in *Howard Barker: a Personal View*, that Barker writes with a:

> calculated poetic syntax, with particular cadences of its own ... each word is an action. He writes with performance energy at the forefront of his consciousness. He is an actor's writer'[74].

While this focus on the author would seem to be the answer to the problems expressed in *The Playwrights' Manifesto*, it creates other, more substantial problems which also relate back to the Manifesto. Barker, in his rejection of popular and, as he sees them, easily accessible art forms such as satire, constructs the language of his plays in way that demands commitment on the part of an audience. His audiences will always have to work hard at understanding his plays.

71. Griffiths, T. R. and Woddis, C. in *Bloomsbury Theatre Guide*. London: Bloomsbury. 1991. p.22.

72. I would draw a distinction between the terms 'popular' and 'populist'. The former being located in, for example, the work of John McGrath and his use of performative forms that are familiar to particular communities — the recognition of a 'folk' culture distinct from the high art of bourgeois culture. The latter term, 'populist', being more concerned with the selling of an art commodity that, in its search for a financial profit, often creates a market/need through, sentimentalised images of a human condition. An equation may be offered: profit motive creates a fashion of the moment: fashion determines values.

73. Shaughnessy, R. 'Howard Barker, the Wrestling School and the Cult of the Author' in *New Theatre Quarterly*. Vol. V No. 19. Cambridge: Cambridge University Press. 1989. p.266.

74. McDiarmid, I. 'Howard Barker: a personal view' in *Gambit*. No. 41. pp.94-6.

> I do think that audiences should have to work on my plays. If they
> don't want to work, then they may as well not be there. It does
> involve commitment ... I think that if you want to learn from the
> theatre, then you have to be committed to it — it's not something
> the writers or the actors have to give to you passively. I like active
> audiences — which is why I'm not a propagandist, because
> propaganda cannot rely upon the conviction of the audience[75].

If we consider the elements involved so far in this equation (the
writer's complex language; being an actor's writer — the language
allowing them to display the full range of their skills; the creation of
The Wrestling School devoted to Barker's *oeuvre* and the demands of
the plays on the audience's level of commitment) a picture emerges
that seems to centralise the author as icon to an even greater degree
than was previously envisaged. This is not the simplistic notion of
'truthful' representation sought after by the playwrights who sue
theatre directors on the grounds of misinterpretation; or at least it
isn't in the sense that they recognise the director's/actor's craft being
at its best when the text is faithfully translated into action. The
implications of *The Wrestling School* are somewhat different. The
writer is perceived as the *auteur* of the whole theatrical process. The
author's language is such that it instructs the actor and allows the
author the privilege of being the sole mediator of meaning. Barker
espouses an elitism in culture; in his view, the only culture that is
viable is owned by the bourgeoisie. That doesn't mean however, that
it should serve the purposes of the bourgeoisie.

While the precise mode of Barker's socialism is hard to define —
necessarily difficult and obscure — it most certainly is there. It is
intrinsic to his concept of culture and the function of theatre in our
society. For Barker, the culture that is elite, is difficult, demanding
commitment of the audience, and is the culture that may effect
change. In a not dissimilar way to Brian Friel, Seamus Heaney and
others in Northern Ireland, Barker is pursuing a belief in the
potential efficacy of art.

> I just think that writers, even if they don't see what their work is
> doing, do produce a testament and I do think that the testament of
> writers is important. You can get a bit mystical about it, but
> somehow the existence of the thing does matter. I just trust it. I trust
> the creation of art[76].

Conclusions

The events in Europe in the 1970s and 1980s have shown that the
seemingly gradual sense of progress, at least believed in, if not an
actuality, was entirely disrupted after the watershed of 1968 and
1969. The governments in Britain and Germany moved to the right,
while the socialist presidency of François Mitterand, elected in May
1981, was unlikely to succeed in its ideals; partly due to its
ideological isolation in Western Europe and partly because the

75. Howard Barker
     interviewed by Finlay
     Donesky.'Oppression,
     Resistance and the
     Writer's Testament' in
     New Theatre Quarterly.
     Vol.II No.8.
     Cambridge:
     Cambridge University
     Press. 1986. pp.336-
     344.

76. Howard Barker
     interviewed *New
     Theatre Quarterly*. Vol.8
     No.II. p.344.

capitalists took their money out of France as soon as he was elected. What price democracy, when the electoral system in Britain means that a political party with fewer people voting for it than for the other parties, may command a huge majority in the parliament. Through all aspects of European life in the 1970s and 1980s, the question of identity would seem to be paramount — nations reaching for new identities after the holocaust of the Second World War; nations (such as Britain) seemingly reaching back for the mythology of an old identity located somewhere in the nineteenth century. Perhaps the most complex case of all is Germany, having been defeated and split asunder, now (at least the western half) finding itself the most financially stable of the European nations, but still without a clear sense of identity in unity.

Identity would seem to be the dominant cultural preoccupation which is commanding our attention. This is operating at a level of national as well as that of personal identity; both left-wing and right-wing ideologies are continuously attempting to redefine themselves. In the theatre, many playwrights feel themselves to be disenfranchised from the 'art' that they create, by the crafts persons they see as being there to interpret. Equally the actors/directors feel themselves oppressed by playwrights and wish to be the central creative force in the process of making theatre. And both writers and actors have reacted against what they perceive as the tyranny of the polemic director, who sees the text as 'merely' a score and the actor as an *über marionette.*

There is a great danger that the positions adopted by writers and perfomers are seen as ideological polarities. There are writers who work closely in collaboration with actors and directors. The task here has been to highlight the points of contention in the complexity of European cultural patterning, as much as it is the purpose of observing moments where substantial co-operation has taken place. The contradicitons that are apparent in working practices are as important as the contradicitions in our daily lives. The value in pointing them out is to challenge simplistic notions that would declare cultural values to be fixed and absolute.

Jack Lang, who was appointed to the top post in the Ministry of Culture by President Mitterand, created controversy by his remarks regarding American cultural imperialism at the 1982 Deauville Film Festival; remarks which he repeated at the UNESCO conference in Mexico City in July 1982. Lang's appointment was a part of Mitterand's socialist agenda, and certainly was an appointment that promised much for the radicalisation of the arts programmes in France. The outcome, inevitably was more complex than had been envisaged, and the problems were intensified by the economic recession developing in Europe and North America.

Jack Lang, quite clearly, was expressing his (and the French) concern that their own identity was being swamped by the new the all-pervasive cultural imperialism of the United States of America. Lang's views are two-edged, for on the one hand he is quite understandably making a stand against the American cultural invasion, but on the other he is engaged with the French pre-occupation with the centrality of French high culture to Europe. It would seem that the move towards a potential European identity is, in part, motivated by the threat of American cultural imperialism; but equally there is a problem of European inter-relationship between national identities, which is exacerbated by individual national relationships with ex-colonial cultures. The problems of post-colonial relationships are a continuing presence, particularly in the work of those theatre practitioners who pursue the concept of the 'other' in the cult of 'orientalism'.

The problem of identity in European culture often hinges on concepts of hierarchy. Hierarchy at a national level as well as hierarchy in working relationships in the theatre. This is clearly shown in reports of working conditions of the French theatre in the 1970s and 1980s and relates to the concept of director as *auteur*. This phenomenon manifests itself in many European cultures, but John Allen reveals evidence of its institutionalised form in France[77]. A discussion had taken place in 1977 at the *Théâtre de Gennevilliers*, a subsidised theatre to the north of Paris. One of the actors expressed the opinion that as long as the actors remained as *sous-traitant du discours dramatique* (a sub-contractor to the dramatic discourse) then nothing will change in the theatre. The director is placed in a hierarchical position in relation to the actor, which reduces the role of the actor to that of an employee, rather than collaborator in the creative process. Apparently this status quo is enshrined in the contracts which are drawn up for young actors and actresses and for directors in many French companies.

> ... the resentment of many young French actors for the director is based on the procedure by which contracts for subsidy are made between the Ministry and the director of the theatre, thus underlining the latter's position of authority ...[78]

Of course, the playwright is not immune from this jostling for position within a hierarchical structure. There have been notable efforts in post-war European theatre to create more democratic (collaborative) structures for the production of theatre, such as the *Joint Stock Theatre Company* in Britain. The aim of companies such as this is to restore (ref. the Elizabethan public theatres) the playwright to the material business of making theatre. The problem for some playwrights is that they do not, in reality, wish for that level of co-operation. Their aim is to retain the status quo whereby the theatre practitioners (directors, actors, designers) all are interpreters of the given literary text; thus recognising the authority of the literary form over the material practice.

The valorisation of the playwright as the *auteur*, as well as author of theatre is a central issue in Western European culture. It is also a part of the broader growth of individualism as an ideology, from the eighteenth century onwards. Certainly, we may argue that it is

77. Allen, J. *Theatre in Europe*. London: City Arts. 1981. p.188.

78. *Ibid*. p.188.

intrinsic to the development of European capitalism, as we may observe when Foucault refers to the point at which we began to recount the lives of authors, rather than those of heroes[79]. Heroes, having no place in the material world of the bourgeoisie, belong to the pre-capitalist stage where power lies in those whose status affords them a semi-mythological persona.

The argument that has been pursued by many theoreticians (perhaps most notably by Roland Barthes as well as Foucault) seeks to determine an answer to the question, 'is the reader or the text the source of meaning?' The movement of the debate has been to dislodge the text (and therefore the author) as the centre of authority. The application of interpretative strategies by the reader, effectively forms the text and gives it cultural shape. The debate is complex, far more so than space in this context allows. However, I bring it into this argument for the purpose of foregrounding the problems to be encountered when the author of the play, not only desires to retain her or his position as sole voice in the text, but, furthermore requires authorship over the theatrical 'reading' of the text. Foucault and others are, in the main, debating the issue of the cultural production of meaning with reference to the literary text.

In theatre there is, beyond that debate, a necessary progression away from the literary object (if the play is to be transformed into theatrical performance) to a potential plurality of positions in the process at which meaning is determined. Again, beyond this process which is to a greater or lesser extent a collective activity, is the point at which a performance text is achieved. At this point there is a 'group' readership that we identify as audience. In this context it may be possible to argue that there are many readings of the theatrical event occurring simultaneously, as each member of the audience receives the (performance) text. Determining the point in theatrical production at which the interpretative strategies give meaning is difficult and more determined by communities and sub-communities of meaning — at every stage of the production process — than it is by individual readings. Quite where we place the sense of ownership of meaning demanded by many playwrights is an engaging problem for our times.

79. Foucault, M. 'What is an Author?' trans. Havari, J.V. 1979 in *Modern Criticism and Theory*. Lodge, D. ed. London: Longman. 1988. p.197.

Around the Fall of the Berlin Wall and the Changing Map of Europe: 1986-1995

In proposing to discuss the development of European theatre in the 1980s and 1990s, it is essential to the task that full cognisance be taken of the whole of Europe and not just the member states of the European Community. If the starting point for this discussion is the effect on European culture of the fall of the Berlin Wall, then it follows that the events in the other Stalinist communist states cannot be ignored. Certainly the career of Václav Havel, from dissident playwright to president of his country, has to be of interest, not only in itself, but also in the ramifications it has for theatre in Western Europe.

From its inception in the 1950s, there has been a movement within the European Community that has urged the consideration of federalism as the ultimate goal for post-war Western Europe. In a world dominated by super powers, such an ambition is understandable, if only on the grounds of protectionism. Not withstanding the fact of the European Community, full federalism as a probability is a long way off. However, what was not predicted in the aftermath of the Second World War was the possibility of a re-emergent nationalism, resulting from the collapse of Stalinism in the Soviet Union and the satellite states of Eastern Europe. Even within the European Community ideas of federalism have yet to supercede the interests of the various nation states. There are many new international organisations that have emerged from the European Parliament, but the interests of the nation state are still paramount.

It would seem that since the Second World War, there have, in effect, been two Europes; the Western capitalist liberal democracies and the communist bloc of Eastern Europe. Even that division of Europe is not entirely accurate, for in the mid-1990s, we are increasingly aware of that other Europe — the one that we refer to collectively as the Balkans. We may pursue the pattern even further if we accept the argument that no power bloc can be considered in isolation. A constant element that has arisen in the discussion on European theatre is the relationship that now exists between Europe and its former colonies — a consideration particularly apposite when we attempt to understand the cultural status quo involved in impetus towards 'interculturalism' in certain theatrical practices.

In the light of the tensions that exist, not only between the states of Western Europe and those of the former Soviet Bloc, but also those tensions between the nation states of Western Europe themselves, we cannot ignore the cultural links and political tensions that exist between the European states and the Islamic world of the Middle East. Even the Arabic community, with its common linguistic and religious heritage, cannot be seen as a single entity. The cultures that comprise the Islamic world of the Middle East span North Africa, the Arabian peninsula, the Fertile Crescent and the non-Arab Middle East in Turkey. The connections are recent and run deep; if only in the fact that Britain and France were largely responsible, after the First World War, for the recent constructs that now make up the Middle Eastern states.

Quite how we define the nature of cultural, as opposed to physical boundaries, is not the intention of this analysis — no more than it has been the intention to include all the cultures of Western Europe in the argument. This is not in any substantial sense a survey. The point has been to construct a series of arguments relating to certain issues in post-war theatre. The examples have been chosen because they usefully represent certain preoccupations, tensions, or indeed interventions in the way that we perceive our cultures. What does seem to unite Europe today is the common uncertainty of its political life. The rapidity of events in the Eastern Bloc, after 1989, took all Europeans by surprise, not least in the different ways that the economic ideologies of the West were adopted with an enthusiasm that took little account of the problems that a free market ideology creates. The ideological confusions for many people sprang from what were, hitherto, clearly defined terms. The Western left-wing revolutionaries of the late 1960s found themselves, in the eyes of many people, representing the last gasp of a now discredited utopia, seen in the lately communist countries as the conservative reactionaries. The aspirants to bourgeois values became the radicals for the future. If a common cause has manifest itself in contemporary Europe, it has been born out of a confusion over the loss of ideological bearings. In Britain this was exemplified by the common oversimplification of the term 'radical'. So often to be 'radical' has carried the assumption that it means *ipso facto* left wing. The shock to many was to realise that Margaret Thatcher represented a radical ideology.

It would seem that many different manifestations of fundamentalism have filled the vacuum created by a loss of clearly defined positions. Across Europe it is easy to find examples of an increase in racism, xenophobia, chauvinism and nationalism as the result of the loss of older certainties (usually the retreat of fascism). No wonder that in the post-modern world we find the cry that there is an end to history. All that is left, it would seem, is the endless recycling of ideas. If Europe is fragmenting into smaller and smaller nation states, confounding what was thought to be the inevitable progress towards federalism, it is a scenario without advocates.

When what may be referred to as the fragmentation of imagery in the twentieth century, when modernism was a force, was the potentiality of a dialectic emerging out of multi-perspective vision offered a new way of seeing and thinking. The writings of Walter Benjamin (*The Work of Art in an Age of Mechanical Reproduction,* in *Illuminations*) and the fragmentation of imagery in Cubism are primary examples. With the post-modern image of recycling and continuous inter-textual self referencing, nothing is offered but a retreat into self-interest. After the Second World War the choices were, and are, not so much a question of liberty or totalitarianism, but more a question of competing political families claiming abandoned territory.

In one sense the Berlin Wall was built at the very moment the Allies met in the final moments of their defeat of Germany at the end of the Second World War. The events that led up to the dismantling of the Wall, apart from the significance embodied in the event itself, revealed a context of significance for the role of theatre in contemporary European culture. Any new order will grow out of the old conditions and find its constituent elements in the past, even if it recasts them in surprising new patterns. I have already referred to the relationship established between art and its political context in the discussion on Brian Friel and *The Field Day Theatre Company*. In Václav Havel, the Czech playwright, we find not only a concrete example of an individual whose position in his culture affords him the role of president of the Czech state[1], but whose role as a dissident playwright also sheds light on the complexity of the artist in relationship to the former regime.

An interest in Havel is not so much promoted by any concept of the valorised author, but more the way by which his actions, as much as his plays and what they say, comments upon the position of the artist in relationship to the political status quo of a repressive regime. It is inevitable that Havel's work was not widely known in the West until his reputation as a dissident was reported. Indeed his plays may not be regarded by many as particularly radical in terms of avant garde theatre in the West, or indeed by the radicalism in form and content of Brecht and his heirs. This in itself is interesting, for it releases us from the necessity to judge art by its seeming radical materialist or subjectively transcendental qualities and forces us to consider the context of its making, as much as any other factor that might be brought to bear in assessment.

Briefly, Havel was born in 1936 and consequently grew up in the Czechoslovakia that was within the Soviet Union's sphere of influence. His background was bourgeois which effectively barred him from studying drama at university. Instead he was required to work his way up through the ranks of manual workers in the theatre, initially as a stagehand, later as a lighting technician and eventually as dramaturg at the Prague theatre on the *Balustrade*. There he began to write plays, initially in what has been termed the 'absurdist' mode[2]. The Russian invasion precipitated by the Prague spring of 1968 resulted in Havel being excluded from participating in theatre work. The *Prague Spring* in itself is an interesting example of the confusion

1. Czechoslovakia ceased to be a single state in 1993 and split into two sovereign nations: The Czech Republic and Slovakia.
2. I hesitate to use the blanket term *Absurd*. There is little substance in the word as a genre in the theatre, the term having been applied by Martin Esslin to a whole range of playwrights in his book *The Theatre of the Absurd*. Penguin. 1961. For many theatre analysts, there is no justification for this over-simplification in reference to many writers of quite disparate ideologies. Reference may be made to Albert Camus' use of the term in *Le Mythe de Sisyphe*.

of what is meant by the radical in European politics. While in 1968
the students and workers in Western Europe were demonstrating on
a largely leftist agenda, the Prague rising was against the Stalinist
regime in Czechoslovakia. There, what passed for socialism was the
force of conservatism, while in the West the ideology of radicalism
was a broadly leftist Marxist movement

After the Russian invasion of 1968, Havel continued to work for
human rights and in 1977 was a founder member of *Charter 77*. In
1979 he was imprisoned by the authorities for his involvement in the
Committee for the Defence of the Unjustly Prosecuted. While seen
as a leading dissident by many people, particularly those outside
Czechoslovakia, Havel himself preferred to see his situation in terms
of 'living in truth'. This is an important distinction and requires
explanation in order for the whole situation to be contextualised and
understood.

The clear result of the political situation in the Eastern Bloc is
that socialism/communism (the conflation of the two terms is so
common as to achieve its own meaning separate from any historical
and theoretical definition) is generally abhorred. It represents the
face of oppression not, as many in the West see it, the way to
liberation. The reaction to the regimes of countries such as
Czechoslovakia has found intelligence in four themes: the recreation
of a civil society; the appeal of 'liberalism'; the obsolescence of the
categories of 'left' and 'right' and the prospect of a third way[3]. In
particular the concept of a 'civil society' occurs most frequently and
represents the attempt to transcend the provincial and destructive
terms of traditional debates. The irony of course here is that those
traditional local antagonisms that existed before the Second World
War, and had been kept under control by the state apparatus of the
communist regime, re-surfaced with depressing rapidity, resulting in
the division of Czechoslovakia into the separate states of the Czech
Republic and Slovakia.

> It (civil society) stood for everything that Communism was not: a
> vision of public affairs in which the place of the state and authority
> was distinct and delimited, in which citizens exercised autonomy
> and occupied a social arena whose various attributes — culture,
> politics, the market in goods — were the outcome of private or
> collective preferences, decided upon by free choice and the balance
> of competing needs and wants. Little attention was paid to the
> distinction between 'civil society' and 'political society', with the
> result that in a curious way the political thought of dissidents
> reversed but did not rethink the very categories and experience of
> Communism itself: just as the Soviet-imposed regimes forbade
> politics but thereby politicised every aspect of daily life, so their
> opponents imagined a counter-society in which politics, in the
> classical sense, would be effectively absent[4].

The free moral world envisaged by Havel turned out to be, after the
events of 1989, populated by many different and conflicting interests.

3. Judt, T. 'Ex Oriente
Lux? Post-Celebratory
Speculations on the
"Lessons" of '89', in
*Towards a Greater
Europe?*. Crouch, C.
and Marquand, D. eds.
Oxford: Blackwell.
1992. pp.91–104.

4. *Ibid.* p.25.

Simple binary structures that attempted to identify, for the common good, where private interest or the collective good lay, were insufficient to deal with the complex pattern of vested interest that has emerged in the early 1990s. The division of Czechoslovakia is evidence enough to make the point. Václav Havel's concept of 'living in truth' is a direct correlative of the 'civil society' in the necessity for the individual to adhere to personal dignity and personal responsibility. In the centralised state control, that Havel perceived in the communist regime, he created what might clearly be seen as an existential choice; his meaning had to be based on the level of personal integrity. However, some of Havel's earliest writings have expressed a form of anti-modernism in their unflinching morality. The generation that had grown up under communism reacted strongly against an ideology that argued that the world could be controlled scientifically by a form of hyper-rationalism. This, in the final analysis, was the original sin of the modern world.

The Vanek plays *Audience, Private View* and *Protest* date from 1975 and deal with an alter-ego of Havel by the name of Ferdinand Vanek. This character has been described by Tom Stoppard (a campaigner on Havel's behalf in the United Kingdom) as 'a doppelganger, a playwright and a persona–non–grata ... whose adventures are sardonically recalled in three short plays'[5]. The plays were intended primarily for audiences in the West, presumably in order to give a sense of Havel's situation to our society. The plays are somewhat short on action, concentrating more on the delineation of character and its relation to society, representing a rejection of crass Western consumerism, as much as they reject scientific totalitarianism as experienced in Stalinist Czechoslovakia.

The Audience, the first of the plays, is set in a brewery where the playwright Vanek now works because he has incurred the disapproval of his government. Although containing only one short act and requiring just two actors, Havel manages to convey the senselessness of a world where disapproval, on a governmental level, can only result in the mistrust and irrational hostility from the rest of society towards the unfortunate individual. Vanek, the playwright, now working in the cellar of the brewery is called to an audience with the Head Malster. The narrative is repetitive and meaningless, relentless in its non-sequiturs: the Head Malster drinks heavily, all the time pressing drinks on the hapless Vanek, who does not wish to drink. The same questions are repeated, not as violent interrogation, but as an indication of the paucity of significance in the life of the Head Malster who has no real power. The only breaks in the narrative are when the Malster goes to relieve himself in the lavatory. On his return the previous scene is re-run with very little change. The significance of the play is only revealed at the end. The Head Malster offers Vanek an easy job in a warm office, only if he will help him report on Vanek's activities to the government. It is at this point that the true impotence of the individual living under an oppressive regime is understood. The irony, in the view of the Malster, is that

5. Havel, V. Introduction to *The Memorandum.* Methuen. 1981

the only person able to escape is the intellectual, because everyone is at least interested in him. This should not be read as a form of post-Hegelian 'spiritual freedom', but more on the material level as expressed, at least he is of interest to the government:

> Who? You! Intellectuals! Gentlemen! just mumbo-jumbo, la-di-da words, that's all you know! And why not? You can afford it! Nothing's ever going to happen to you! Everybody's interested in you! You know all the angles! You know how to stick up for yourselves! You're up even when you're down! But an ordinary bloke's just got to carry on! And what's the good of all this drudgery?

The *dénouement*, if *dénouement* it be, is after Vanek leaves the audience with the Malster. He then returns, the Malster is sober once more and the play clearly is about to be re-run. The difference is that Vanek is now assertive and wanting the drink offered, delivering the final line of the play as: 'Eh, screw it all! The lot!'

In some ways the strong sense of the morality of 'living in the truth' is concerned with returning Europe to a common cultural heritage, while having little to do with the contemporary ideas of European federalism. It has much to do with a pre-Enlightenment moral heritage that takes the form of a critique of modernity in general. In this, Václav Havel may be seen very much as the East European whose social vision — of necessity — goes beyond what he may perceive as the idle speculations of his Western counterpart. As may be discerned in the brief observations on *The Audience*, Havel has little more time for the contemporary intellectual position in the West, than he does for the oppression of Stalinism. He views politics, that is 'genuine' politics in his terms, as a matter of service:

> ... the only politics I am willing to devote myself to — is simply a matter of serving those around us: serving the community, and serving those who will come after us. Its deepest roots are moral because it is a responsibility, expressed through action, to and for the whole, a responsibility that is what it is — a 'higher' responsibility — only because it has a metaphysical grounding ... [6]

Heiner Müller

I shit
on the order of the world
I am
lost[7].

Heiner Müller's second excursion into directing — after his career had been concerned largely with writing — could been read as a metaphor for the destruction of the Berlin Wall and the unification of Germany. In 1990 Müller directed the *Hamlet/Machine* which was

6. Havel, V. *Summer Meditations on Politics, Morality and Civility in a Time of Transition.* trans. Wilson, P. London: Faber. 1992. p.6.
7. Müller, H. ' Fatzer+/-Keuner' in Essays on German Theater. trans. Agee, J. Herzfeld-Sander, M. ed. New York: Continuum. 1985. from Rotwelsch. Berlin. 1982.

the result of an integration of Shakespeare's *Hamlet* (second Quarto) and his own *Hamlet* experiment, the montage, *Hamletmachine*. *Hamletmachine* reflects upon Shakespeare's play and its focus on the transition between the feudal world of 'old Hamlet' and the new despotic (Tudor) world of Claudius — the transition from the old tragic revenge play of the 1580s and Shakespeare's reworking of the theme in his *Hamlet*. The production occurred just after the fall of the Berlin Wall and marked the end of the German Democratic Republic. Many critics referred to the *Hamletmachine* as 'a state funeral' for the passing of the old Stalinist state, while marking the insecurity of what was on offer in the unification with the 'shop window' of the West.

Heiner Müller is perhaps the apposite paradigmatic figure through which to consider the condition of contemporary European culture. The first point is the most obvious: he is German. Apart from the accepted centrality of Germany in contemporary Europe, the position occupied by Müller in the (then) two Germanies serves as an interesting key to the purpose. Müller the writer has been the recipient of prestigious literary prizes from both the post-war Germanies. From the Federal Republic was awarded both the Mülheim and the Büchner literary prizes, and from the German Democratic the National Prize — a *Werkschau* where international theatre workers and scholars gathered in Berlin to discuss different aspects of his work. Whereas it is possible to argue that Václav Havel, the other significant theatrical element in the 'velvet revolution' of the late 1980s, sought a mode of moral living that reached back to pre-Enlightenment consciousness, Müller is to be located very much in contemporary debates regarding the function of culture.

With the division of Germany in the aftermath of the Second World War, Müller's family chose to move to the West, while Müller stayed in East Berlin. Like Bertolt Brecht, with whom Müller is often associated, he has occupied an ambiguous relationship with the Stalinist regime, seeking new forms (or deconstructing old ones) as a means of articulating a sense of the 'nuclear' age. In many senses, Müller's work is focused on the development of German culture in the nineteenth and twentieth centuries. Three names occur frequently as 'fathers' of Müller's work, although he is just as likely to declare them 'mothers' and, without doubt, he has moved away from them all in different ways. Clearly Bertolt Brecht was important, as was Georg Büchner, in the fragmentary form by which we have received *Woyzeck*. The third 'father' is Vladimir Mayakovsky, particularly in his deliberate deconstruction of all forms of literary rules, with the aim of achieving a new revolutionary poetic vigour. The problem is understanding the sum of Müller's work, when there is not any sum (form) or linear narrative to be easily attained. In the early 1970s when Müller broke with many traditions (linear narrative) and easy consistency in language structure, each new piece of writing, and latterly directing, has established a different style and perspective. Perhaps one way to understand the fragmentary perspective of Müller, and thus to gain a sense of his location in the structure of contemporary European cultures, is by reference to Müller's essay *Fatzer +/- Keuner*[8].

The essay deals, in particular, with a critique of Brecht, contextualising his position, and by implication delineating the problems in contemporary art. For Müller, historical circumstances forced Brecht into the dilemma of classicism. The argument is based on the historical circumstances of Germany, initially failing to have the bourgeois revolution of France and Britain, thus forcing the emergence of the Weimar classic period as 'a neutralisation of the positions of the *Sturm und Drang*'. He further argues that one of the great misfortunes of recent (twentieth-century) history was the failure of the proletarian revolution in Germany. The consequent establishment of a Soviet-dominated estate, under conditions of deprivation in the post-war period, inevitably led to the socialist experiment developing in isolation.

Müller's argument in reference to Brecht, centres on Brecht adopting a form of classicism in his use of the parable as a narrative form in his plays. The direct cause is outlined by Müller:

> Brecht's expulsion from Germany, his distance from the German
> class struggles , the impossibility of continuing his work in the Soviet
> Union meant emigration into classicism. His Versiche 1-8 contains
> the vital part of his work, as far as its potential for immediate
> political impact is concerned — its theological core of fire, in the
> sense of Walter Benjamin's conception of Marxism. Hollywood
> became the Weimar of the German anti-fascist emigration. The need
> not to talk about Stalin — because his name stood for the Soviet
> Union so long as Hitler was in power — compelled the exiles to
> resort to generalities: hence the parable form[9].

It is in the generality of the parable form as exploited by Brecht, that Müller sees the link with Weimar classicism. The parable has specific points of reference from which it may take its bearings and thus retain its links to a concept of reality rooted linear progression, despite Brecht's employment of the episodic structure in his plays. The implication is that episodic structure in dramatic/theatrical form does not necessarily carry the same radical potentiality as montage — the juxtaposition of dissimilars. Müller refers to a discussion between Brecht and Walter Benjamin on the subject of Kafka. The point that Benjamin makes is based on the idea that Kafka's use of parable is more 'capacious' than Brecht's. Kafka's model portrays gestures without necessarily giving them any specific frame of reference; they are not reducible to any single meaning. This is, he argues, because the image in Kafka is alien, rather than alienating in the sense of *Verfremdung* as exploited by Brecht.

It seems that Müller is pursuing a course of action that ultimately leads to a rejection of rationalism; certainly rationalism related to ideas of 'Enlightenment'. Within this broad framework the attitude towards Brecht is not so much one of rejection, as seeing the need

8. *Ibid*
9. *Ibid*. pp.338-339.

for re-assessment. Without doubt the ideas, arguments and practices of Bertolt Brecht have been much appropriated and, simultaneously, abused by Western European theatre practitioners[10]. Our problem with Brecht, is that he has been valorised, and his work has been institutionalised into the canon of great European art; the slight problem raised by his politics is usually dealt with by a declaration that, at the heart of the matter there is a great poet whose art ultimately transcends the Marxism of his politics[11]. Heiner Müller refers to a production of *St Joan of the Stockyards*, where the director felt that it was important to, 'obscure what Brecht had clarified, so that it could be seen anew':

> On every territory that has yet been occupied by the Enlightenment, unknown zones of darkness have 'unexpectedly' opened up. Again and again the alliance with rationalism has exposed the Left to back-stabbing by the powers of reaction, with daggers that were always forged in these zones of darkness. What has been recognised is not well known ... To use Brecht without criticising him is to betray him[12].

The so-called post-modern world of Europe is a difficult concept with which to come to terms, and certainly this is one writer who would gladly support legislation to outlaw the term in its more reactionary manifestations. However, if we refer to Müller's work as post-modern and if we also refer to him as one of the more interesting and complex leftist writers and directors to emerge from the communist bloc, quite what do we mean?

Does post-modernism mean the end of history in a rationalist sense? Is it indeed possible to approach a definition in those terms? Does not the 'state of post-modernism' necessarily mean that those categories of questions are inappropriate, and belong to an ideology that is already defunct in the libertarian free market of textual meanings? At the base line the implication is that there are no new things to say and texts can now only be self-and inter-referential. Certainly, that is how many people read the contemporary human condition. However, for Müller the function of art is a far more complex business. For him, and many other contemporary leftist artists, the re-assessment of Brecht and others of that generation does not mean that the business of politics is neglected. The point is particularly apposite when we recognise the post–colonial state of contemporary Europe. Müller remarks:

> I cannot keep politics out of the question of post-modernism. Periodisation is the politics of colonialism as long as history has as its prerequisite the domination of elites through money or power and does not become universal history which has as its prerequisite real equal opportunity. Perhaps that which predated modernism will reappear in other cultures in a different way, albeit enhanced by the technological progress of modernism influenced by Europe: a social realism which helps to close the gap between art and reality[13].

10   See McCullough, C. 'Brecht and brechtian: estrangement and appropriation' in *The Politics of Theatre and Drama*. Holderness, G. ed. London: Macmillan. 1992.

11. More recent methods of de-politicising Brecht and his works have found voice in Feugi, J. *The Life and Lies of Bertolt Brecht* London: Harper Collins. 1994. Feugi's thesis that Brecht merely exploited a number of women by seducing them and getting them to write his plays does no justice to anyone; least of all the intelligent women who were Brecht's communist collaborators. See also Esslin, M; Bentley, E. et al.

12. *op cit.* Müller. pp.340-344.

13. Müller, H. 'Reflections on Post-modernism' New York: Continuum. 1985. pp. 346. Originally in *New German Critique*. No.16. Winter 1979. trans. Zipes, J.

Müller while recognising that art, like New York, constitutes itself out its decay[14], still needs to shape itself in some way that addresses an audience, not from a perspective of privilege, but from commonality. Müller's work has undergone many transformations, from his work influenced by Büchner, Brecht and Mayakovsky, to reworking Classics, and to directing his own reworkings of his plays. The constant element is rooted in his inconsistency. With each new experiment there is a rejection (or re-evaluation) of a past technique intrinsic to the constantly shifting ideologies of identity in Europe. The loss of clearly defined identities requires an art that no longer deals in consistencies of form or content. It is no longer, as it was with Brecht, Piscator and their contemporaries, the task of developing new forms for the new ideas of revolution. The nature of the revolution in a post cold war era is no longer clearly defined. The future is no longer clear and Müller recognises, in his more recent work, that the future cannot be patriarchal. This is a subject that I have deliberately avoided addressing directly, not out of hostility, but out of a recognition that it is inappropriate for men to pronounce on the potential of this way forward. Nevertheless, it is worth quoting, as a postscript, Ophelia's speech from Müller's *Hamletmachine*.

> OPHELIA: *While two men in white smocks wrap gauze around her and the wheelchair, bottom to top.*
>
> This is Electra speaking. In the heart of darkness. Under the sun of torture. To the capitals of the world. In the name of the victims. I eject all the sperm I have received. I turn the milk of my breasts into lethal poison. I take back the world I gave birth to. I choke between my thighs the world I gave birth to. I bury it in my womb. Down with the happiness of submission. Long live hate and contempt, rebellion and death. When she walks through your bedrooms carrying butcher knives you'll know the truth.
>
> *The men exit. Ophelia remains on stage, motionless in her white wrappings.*

Conclusions

In no way has this volume attempted a detailed study of all the significant theatre practitioners in post-war Europe. It should be clear from what has been tackled, that there is no longer any sure way by which a person, or a theatrical practice, may be determined as 'significant'. Perhaps the only certainty in post-colonial modern Europe is the uncertainty apparent to the many people who seek identities not based on exploitation. The two contemporary examples of Václav Havel and Heiner Müller represent two responses coming from what many of us in the politically determined western part of the continent, the 'other' Europe. Havel's sense of 'living in the truth' has produced an identity that seeks to give itself voice through older certainties. Heiner Müller, also of that 'other' Europe,

14. *Ibid.* p.347.

recognises the end of one history, but distinguishes himself and his work by continuously seeking new relationships and structures by which we may articulate our condition. He is at odds with the post-modern condition. In his own words, his role is not:

> ... of Polonius, the first comparatist in dramatic literature, last of all in his dialogue with Hamlet about the shape of a certain cloud which demonstrates the real misery of power structures in the very misery of comparison[15].

Postscript

A headline in the Arts pages of *The Guardian* (Monday, May 8, 1995) read 'IN THE STORM OF A DIVIDED SELF'. The subsequent article and review posed a question regarding the contemporary German playwright, Botho Strauss, and his political affiliations. The sub-heading read, 'Drama for German Reactionaries?' Botho Strauss, who is well known in Germany, but virtually unheard of in Britain (which usually may be taken to mean as much a comment on this country's insularity, as it is a comment on the artist) is at the centre of a bitter debate about, 'political correctness, press freedom and the rise of new nationalism'[16]. Strauss has, for many years been a scourge of bourgeois values, both in his prodigious output and his association as translator and adapter with the *Schaubühne's* director Peter Stein. Without doubt Strauss is a formidable man of letters and his apparently renown opaque prose style would seem to be one of the problems at the root of the current controversy.

Strauss who, as well as being a playwright, has been co-editor of *Theater Heute*, published an article in the German weekly news magazine *Der Spiegel* in which, as *The Guardian* reported:

> ... he appeared to blame the post-war liberal establishment for the rise in right-wing violence in Germany. He also seemed to hint that right-wing attacks on foreigners had a 'sacral', ritualistic quality and that they could serve as a cleansing process for society[17].

The article was given the benefit of the doubt, largely on the grounds that no one could be certain that there was not a very sophisticated thesis being prosecuted. However, recent developments have created a situation where Stauss neither confirms, nor denies sympathies with various right-wing groups of intellectuals. His reply, when asked if he would clarify his attitude to a collection of essays expressing right-wing nationalistic views, was to say that he had no objection to it and that none of the essays was quite as 'objectionable' as his own. Subsequently, Stauss has become (been appropriated as?) a hero to many right-wing groups. Others see Strauss more 'as a victim of intellectual hysteria'. The article quotes a view expressed by Gert Voss, a German actor, that echoes statements in the work of Heiner Müller, articulating the very shifting scale of values in the depressing search for a European identity.

15. *Ibid.* p.346.
16. Staunton, D. *The Guardian*. 8 May, 1995.
17. Staunton, D. *The Guardian*. 8 May, 1995. Subsequent references in quotation marks are from this source.

It's a phenomenon here in Germany that since the collapse of socialism left-wingers have started hitting out at other left-wingers and branding them rightists. It is a German sickness and by doing so they are strengthening the right.

The drive towards the creation of the European Community is, without doubt, a part of the effort by Europeans to create a new identity in a world that no longer recognises the Europeans' own sense of inalienable right to power. In this context, the personal issues are very much as political as the public ones. If anything is at all clear, we are in the process of a painful, but necessary reconstruction of our personal and (broadly speaking) cultural identities. In the theatre, this is as much to do with the economics of material working relationships, as it is with what is said, and how it is said.